unununimim
imdededesign

Joannette van der Veer (ed.)

un
n
in
de
des

un-in-design

im
de
es

un un un im imim ~de ~de ~design – or: how ~to un-bake a ~cake

Joannette van der Veer (ed.)

When I Google searched the question 'can you unbake bread?' I stumbled upon an article on SciSnack—a platform that encourages young and early career scientists to improve their writing skills—that drew parallels between scientific models and the baking of cakes. The article gave the example of wanting to replicate a cake for which you do not have the recipe. It read: 'Like many natural processes in science, baking a cake is an irreversible process; once the ingredients are mixed up and baked, there is no going back.'[1] Besides the fact that I am, myself, a baking enthusiast, I found the article an interesting read because it made me consider how so many design processes are still being reproduced. After its fabrication, a cake can only be eaten as much as a design can only be consumed. And even though we have an abundance of (bio)degradable or recyclable materials and products, most of the time these can only be degraded or re- or upcycled by adding something else to the mix. You can unbake a cake as much as you can degrade non degradable plastics—a.k.a you simply cannot.

But there was something else in the article that sparked my interest. In describing the wish to reverse an irreversible process, the author of the SciSnack article mentioned that, indeed, we cannot simply unbake a cake, yet what we can do instead is to bake a lot of cakes, in order to "guess" what ingredients are in the cake that we wish to disentangle and (re)create. Perhaps you wish to alter the recipe to your own taste or liking—more fluffiness, less chocolate, no artificial flavouring, or the adding of sprinkles—which will be a challenging endeavor as cake recipes are delicate: forgetting an ingredient or swapping a step within the process can completely ruin your cake. The process of unbaking, or reversing a (seemingly) irreversible process, is therefore bound to come with a lot of trial and error.

Recently, it has come to my attention that a lot of 'unbaking' has been happening within the realm of design education and discourse. Many a theorist, educator and student ate the design cake that had been baked for them and just did not like the taste of it anymore — they were fed up. Now, in order to bake a cake that is different from the one they were served, it is evidently unavoidable to bake a lot of cakes to see what ingredients they would keep, add, increase, decrease or completely leave out of their own recipe. The result? A very messy kitchen. And that is exactly what today's design field feels like; a sticky counter full of dripping whisks, cake-crusted pans, used spoons, smudged measuring cups and sticky scales.

     Over the past few years, design (discourse) has been learned and unlearned, done and undone, patriarchised and depatriarchised, colonized and decolonized, centralized and decentralized, and so forth. Meanwhile, (departments of) schools, institutions and other bodies within design (education) are wandering, unstable, not-yet, unsettling, or impermanent, making way for anything other than sturdiness.

For example, in 2016, the Dirty Art Department of the Sandberg Instituut hosted the project 'The Wandering School' during Milan Design Week. The project ran a series of events and was presented as a living experimentation that allowed for both success and failure.[2] In 2018, The 4th Istanbul Design Biennial 'A School of Schools' presented itself as a multi-platform biennale that would use, test and revise a variety of educational strategies to 'reflect on the role of design, knowledge and global connectedness in contemporary Istanbul and beyond.'[3] In that same year, the intra-curricular initiative 'Unsettling Rietveld/Sandberg' was brought to life to 'unsettle the Rietveld and Sandberg from the roots up, supporting existing initiatives, while also developing outreach programs, drawing in new perspectives, and making the context of the academy more inclusive to other voices, minds and bodies.'[4] In 2019, the publication 'The Critical Makers Reader' by Loes Bogers and Letizia Chiappini (eds.) delved into the (un)learning of technology, and in 2020 the publication 'Design Dedication' by Annelys de Vet (ed.) made a plea for adaptive mentalities in design pedagogy whilst exploring a myriad of attitudes in and towards design education. More recently, in 2021 the publication 'Glossary of Undisciplined Design' by Anja Kaiser and Rebecca Stephany (eds.) appeared in which undisciplinarity is activated as a feminist unpacking of the graphic design discipline and its structures, canons, teachings, tools and practice. The list of examples goes on.[5]

It seems as if everyone is collectively trying to unbake the cake that is design education and discourse. These acts of undoing and unlearning create a certain pause, a hesitation, a halt, a stutter, a moment to (re)consider what should be said and, most of all, what should be done. The question then presents itself: if all within design is being undone, unmade, unlearned, what is it exactly that is being done, being made, and being learned? This publication and its eponymous 3-day symposium offer a view from within and upon design education and discourse by means of six different 'case studies' that reflect upon the current state of continuous questioning and interrogation in which design actively resides today. It is not meant as an extensive overview, but instead as a collection of insights into the diverse views, ideas, reflections and questions that design practitioners and educators are dealing with today.

It has become very clear that the ways in which design has been doing and has been made, done and learned is outdated. Its formerly set conditions, ideals and modes no longer adhere to the reigning ideas, ethics, questions, and morals of today's (design) society that ask for progressive inclusivity, diversity, transparency, responsibility and accountability from all parties involved—designer, academy, historian, theorist, educator, student, and other "bodies" within that society alike. Therefore, all the efforts being made to unmake or undo seem very much needed and necessary. However, how can we move forward when we are currently concentrating on undoing, unmaking, imagining, imposing, improvising, displacing, designing and de-signing? Why must design be brought to this halt, this full stop? Is it to end design's sentence? Or, on the contrary, to start a new chapter (or full book?) on design altogether?

    This halting state in which design seems to be residing is anything but in stasis, it is very much alive and activated. Mobile, even. Kicking, perhaps. In a way, in its seeming stagnation, the development of design education and discourse appears to have never been more active as it is now. In fact, it can be compared to the act of baking a lot of cakes, people are experimenting with educational tools, different teaching techniques, various modes of making and doing, forms of curriculum, disrupting institutionally embedded hierarchies, all to try and find their ideal recipe. Now, instead of trying to fabricate a cake recipe that is to all our liking within this book, I decided to invite a selection of designers, theorists, curators and educators—from both within and outside of academy and/or university doors—to reflect upon their own ingredients and the messy kitchens they are working in. I would like you to consider this collection of essays/reflections as a cabinet of spices—with one being more outspoken than the other, but all adding something; not just to the cake itself, but to its very unbaking.

    Now, before touching upon this publication's contributions, there is something I wish to mention beforehand. At the very start, this project was called "unununimimimdededesign—a stuttering design discourse". However, along the process of organizing, I experienced a lot of discomfort with the project's title when in dialogue with invited participants and, ultimately, myself. Some invitees did not want to participate altogether because of it, others opened a conversation and suggested reconsidering the title, and a few thought that the stutter metaphor— if being used respectfully—was not an issue at all. These divergent views really stuck with me, like a very sticky batter. They confronted me with my own privilege, biases and faults-by-design, and it appeared as if I had to fulfill the act of unununimimimdededesigning myself first before anything else. In the end, I chose to change the project's and publication's eponymous (sub)title. And yet, I was hesitant to erase the stutter reference and its discomfort from this book altogether. The erasure of a valuable lesson from a book on (design) education was not only incongruous; it felt unfair to do so. Therefore, there are two friendly reminders of the lesson learnt in this book. One reminder being Alice Twemlow's contribution, which offers a critical perspective on the matter. The other reminder being the "Stotts" typeface used throughout this publication; a script developed by graphic designer Lot Mars that offers insight into the complexities of stuttering.

     We start this publication with 'Voice Notes on Uhm-Learning', a contribution by Saskia van Stein and Nadine Botha in close collaboration with students from the MA Critical Inquiry Lab at the Design Academy Eindhoven. Rather than policing or glossing out the bridge word 'uhm', as we so often do in slick presentation style, van Stein and Botha propose to lean and feel into the roles it plays in expanding performative ideas and speech acts. Although the choice to focus on the bridge word 'uhm' came from a misreading of the title of this project—it had been (mistakenly) understood as 'uhmuhmuhm'—the result could not have been more responsive to the publication's theme and framework. The contribution can be read as a timely document on hesitancy within the context of language, communication and design (education).

      With the essay 'Wait for it…', Alice Twemlow critically addresses the 'tempting trap' of metaphoric thinking in relation to stuttering and, more specifically, in relation to the subject matter of this very publication and its used typeface. Twemlow's piece discusses the usage of paratextual elements and typographical experiments by several authors from various eras, whilst reflecting upon silence within an art and design education context. If anything, the contribution allows for inward-looking and self-reflection within this publication at hand as well as a wider design (educational) framework.

    Continuing to touch upon the act of self-reflection is Imad Gebrayel's contribution 'The Design Exit: Don't look back!'. Gebrayel's piece repositions design outside of the art-school system (within the context of the European Union) and discusses the overdue critical 'turn' in design education as a form of alter-reality. According to Gebrayel, the design field is in need of a shift into a new era, away from solutionism and design-positivism. To allow for new figurations of design, Gebrayel suggests it might be time for design (education) to break out of its art and design academy bubble.

Instead of focusing on content, references, canon, assignments and evaluations—as might be expected when discussing discourses around design education—Maya Ober decides to pay attention to the intimate and affective relations that exist between teachers and students within and outside of the classroom. With 'Affective classroom: on choosing life, vulnerability and weakness in design education', Ober discusses the (dis)connection between the body and the classroom from both an analytical as well as highly intimate, personal perspective. Her contribution allows for a critical discussion of homogeneous structures and Euro-patriarchal and modernity-driven logic that exists within, and dominates design education, whilst advocating for more vulnerability, visibility, in the presence of bodies to resist that very framework.

The conversation with Belle Phromchanya and Darunee Terdtoontavedeej (founders of Non Native Native) delves into ideas surrounding authenticity, adaptation and accessibility in relation to living, working, designing and teaching (design) within the Dutch cultural scene and beyond. Each of the duo's personal journeys, as well as collective efforts and experiences with Non Native Native, are being discussed whilst touching upon unsettling relationships, issues of racism and censorship, reclaiming unclaimed spaces and breaking down institutional barriers. In doing so, Phromchanya and Terdtoontavedeej provide room to think about alternative learning spaces that (co-)exist alongside more institutionalized ones.

We close this series of reflective contributions with 'A disappointing bibliography' by Teaching Design (Lisa Baumgarten and Judith Leijdekkers). Inspired by Sarah Ahmed's "survival toolkit for feminist killjoys" in *Living A Feminist Life* (2017), Teaching Design provides us with a list of (re)sources that accompanied the platform's journey within the realm of design education over the years. Let their disappointing list be an encouragement to us all to collectively meet, learn and further expand, explore and examine the field of design (education) and its discourse.

Together, what these reflective contributions demonstrate is that it appears you cannot make a bibliography without exclusion, send a voice note without audible hesitation, or allow for fresh perspectives whilst operating from the same, comfortable viewpoint. In other words, you can't have your cake and eat it too. And that may precisely be the point of this book. We can't change the course of design education and discourse without killing its so-called 'darlings'. And we can't try out different modes of thinking and doing without allowing for discomfort, vulnerability and failure. The book you are holding aims to reflectively pause and build upon the knowledge, thoughts, hesitations, and discomfort that was shared by email, through Zoom calls, and during the three unununimimimdededesign online symposium events held in the summer of 2021. If anything, this book is a very sticky batter

for you to taste, untangle and whisk your way around its viscosity.

1 https://www.scisnack.com/2017/06/07/how-to-unbake-a-cake-or-reverse-an-irreversible-process-in-science/

2 http://wanderingschool.com/

3 http://aschoolofschools.iksv.org/en/#section-new-about-detaillink

4 https://rietveldacademie.nl/en/page/9481/unsettling-rietveld-sandberg

5 Other examples include BAK's Training for the Not Yet program and the Decolonising Design group

→table

→c

of
contents

9
introduction
joannette
van der veer

35
voice notes on uhm-learning
—saskia van stein and nadine —botha

51
wait for it
alice —twemlow

61

the design exit: don't look behind
imad gebrayel

75 affective classroom: on choosing life, vulnerability and weakness in design education —maya ober (—depatriarchise design)

85

reclaiming the unclaimed

a conversation between belle phromchanya, darunee terdtoontaveedej and joannette van der veer

107
a disappointing bibliography teaching design

115 biographies

125 colophon

voice notes on uhm-learning

Saskia van Stein
and Nadine Botha

Voice Notes on Uhm-learning

15 Critical Inquirers start a Signal group to listen to each other's uhms, during this thing we call uhm the global pandemic, and what happens next is uhm post-design, uhm, or is it post de-sign?

1   "As hierarchies are being deconstructed and histories unpacked, we're left without a clear view on the role design and its discourses could have, and how they could be shaped around another set of values, methods and uncertain outcomes. At the heart of Western Eurocentric modernity and market-driven design is a sense of urgency, accompanied by affordable commodities and solutionism. However, in order for the deep-seated structural changes that are being called for to take place, we need to move slower, stay with the discomfort and give ourselves some time to hold the complexity and vocabulary of a currently inarticulable and unconceived reality. Why act or speak if we don't know how to proceed? What might a post-design discipline be? What might be the attitude and vocabulary that you have developed as a (post) design practitioner to navigate starting out in a discipline that has not yet been defined?"

2   ...and send. The email had emerged after a few weeks of video calls, voice notes and email exchanges between Saskia van Stein and Nadine Botha, regarding the upsurge of un-, in- and de- prefixes in the critical discourse of design. Prefixes that counter the initial intent of words and change their direction, coinciding with a broader cultural movement in which history and reality itself are being scrutinised and rewritten. Between a lazily eyed email and a muffled voice note, the un-in-de became constructively misread as uhm, which became the

generative seed of an asynchronous hyperspatial workshop. The email was an invitation to students and alumni of the Critical Inquiry Lab to participate in this workshop, taking place over the course of a few days as people dropped in and out of a Signal group that used voice notes to explore the language of design and the dithering nature of the present by listening and leaning into the word "uhm".

> 3 "...um, um, indeed, uh, where, where to start with this question of words and language. Um..."

4 Despite being widely regarded as a speech error, any serious Scrabble player will be all too happy to explain that um is indeed a word (although the keenest of Scrabble players will notice that "uhm" is technically not a word). According to research women say um more than men, but men are more inclined to say uh than um.[1] So how to deal with such discrepancies of spelling and expression in accordance with different genders? For the purposes of this essay we have chosen to combine uh and um into a *uhm*. Uhm might be defined as an expression of hesitation, doubt, deliberation or interest, depending on its context and usage, however its meaning is by necessity evasive. It is less of a word that transmits content, than a word that performs a function. A literal performative speech act that, according to psychologists, functions to allow the brain to catch up with the mouth, and/or to hedge social and argumentative expectations.[2] Through the use of uhm, there is a buying of time and stretching of temporality, as well as a dithering or negotiating between positions—all qualities that have become egregious to capitalist efficiency and

design's pageantry, of both the critical and airbrushed persuasion. Yet, most of us uhm all day, and we barely notice others', nor our own uhms. What does this word that is an (in)action hiding in plain sight add to an expanding lexicon of post-design and what else might such a language need?

5   "Hrrrrrum Huuum Theee~uuuurm"

6   "Mhmm mhmm mhmm"

7   "Ehkhkhkh aeeehkhkhkh eeeehkhkh"

8   "AHh OHh ah / AHh OHh ah"

9   "_~eh! ...uh uM 'uhm oHm"

10   "uummmm ummm ahhhh ahhhhhh arummm ummmm ahhhhh ahhhh ahhh ah ah ah"

11   "Patakapatakapatakapaaa Patakapatakapatakapaaw patakapatakapatakapooo patakapatakapatakapeeee patakapatakapatakapaay"

12   "Tsik' huum - tskik' hooooum"

13   Was that a giggle!? Were the Signal workshop participants not taking the assignment of re-saying and making-bigger someone else's uhm, and then writing it down in a text message, seriously!? Indeed, what seemed like a sluggish start of tentative introductions, maybe even a sleeper—you know, just another digital workshop where many signed up, less show up and no one opens up—warmed up into a heaving, panting, frothy slew of vowel sounds, barely covering the sniggers and giggles. As we mirrored and were mimicked by each other we

Saskia van Stein & Nadine Botha

were vulnerable, but the opacity of the voice-only medium provided some safety through the illusion of invisibility. Inviting and celebrating our own and each other's uhms, otherwise socially and professionally perceived as glitch--es, empowered by the performative act of not knowing, of uhm. Uhm is play.

14 "...It's nice to hear your voice..."

15 Uhm is #nomakeup #nofilter #behindthescenes. Uhm is the glimpse of the desktop chaos we see in video meetings. Uhm is intimate. Perhaps we forgot to mention upfront, because it's become so pervasive as to seem almost cliched, but this all went down late in the second Dutch lockdown, when the sense between regulation and self-determination, between inside and outside, forward and backward was no longer discernible. No longer was it simply that our language was constrained by wavering prefixes, or that our design discourse was chasing its own tale (sic), but our very material reality and history was in a giant uhm. It was a time when digital messages, mostly text, were all that was keeping us connected to each other, and we had come to loathe our love for the single tick, double tick, blue tick. The only voices most of us heard were those of the family, colleagues and friends closest to us, and the generic media celebrities and anonymous Tiktoks furthest away. The Signal voice note let these other, unrehearsed, self-dubious voices into our beds in the morning, took us on walks in the forest, and on train rides across Europe.

16 "...Sorry for being late. Good afternoon, because it's actually afternoon already"

17 By listening for each other's uhms, hesitancies and not knowing, as something generative, rather than policing each other's critical thought, we also listened more closely to everything else in the voice note other than what was being said. From the bird song to the pub sounds in the background, to each other's drawling accents and peculiar pronunciations, from the temporalities with which we speak, even when communicating asynchronously, to simply hearing each other's voices 'dressing' the words. The voice note itself, in contrast to the constructed, over-mediated text message, or the video call masked by the self-view, is an uhm. A quantum of communication through which the inability to commit to a decisive text message could convey a thought that was being unpacked, thought out loud, or thought in collaboration with the careful consideration of the other listeners. What happens when a thought is externalised?

18 "..., um, when, uh, you talked about the fact that, uh, in a way, just to an externalizing extent, uh, just to say the word, uh, externalize an idea, uh, is already a design..."

19 Language is the dominant reproduction device of our power relations, upbringings and cultures. What we say is how we think, which determines our behaviour and defines our identity. Functioning across the grandest levels of metaphysics and statecraft, to the most interpersonal love poems and inner dialogues, language feels like the biggest system in which each of us still has at least a vestige of immediate and personal agency when the rest of the world has become entirely mediated and controlled. We see this fixation on using the

correct words across the spectrum, from self-help to social justice movements, from left to right politics. It is indicative of the plasticity of language and our brains. That by expanding the set of words and grammars for different genders, sexualities, races and ethnicities, how we perceive and relate to these things evolves. The concomitant resistance to being forced to use certain words and grammars might be explained by knowing just how powerful language is. Words are categories, are technologies, are designs. The words "ozone hole" first used in 1984, designed a concept around which an environmental movement emerged. "Anthropocene" continues to cause quibbles across the spectrum, but as Kathryn Yusoff points out,[3] the word itself is the result of a legacy of the geo-logic that emerged with colonialism to describe black lives as an extractive resource. In our current era in which the data industrial complex absorbs and self-replicates words faster than we can speak them, words like "woke" and "me too", that have bolstered dedicated resistances, quickly become appropriated and commodified. In other words, we are not the only ones who listen to our voice notes. What does the data industrial complex hear and replicate?

20 "...what it takes, all it takes to make the description a true one is the impulse to use it in the first person. And that anyone's use of about themselves means differently from their use of it, about someone else…"

21 Unless you are very familiar with the book, you might not at first notice that there is something off with the automated Rev.com, voice-to-text transcription of a voice note reading a

quote from The Argonauts by Maggie Nelson.[4] The machine listening technology did not hear the use of the word queer twice in the above sentence. These omissions change a quote about how queer is only true when used in the first person, into a quote implying that anything said in the first person is true. Voice-to-text software is based on a predictive machine learning algorithm that has parsed masses of other voice data. Presumably the pronunciation of queer was not registered as a word, and the predictive algorithm completed the sentence based on the most likely way words follow each other. This digital archaeological artefact not only speaks volumes about the dominant order of words, but also the dominant way of saying and hearing. How we say things can radically alter the transmissibility and significance of language. How we say things cannot necessarily be spelt or heard in a universal way—consider the different sounds and spellings of uhm in notes 5–12.

22 "And I am aware of the fact that I'm pr-... I pronounced the same word wrongly, but I like it because my dyx... dyslexia, uh, subverts the word itself and I, I am embracing it, uh, as a welcome error."

23 What the Maggie Nelson quote also introduced to the conversation is the upsurge in autobiography, autoethnography and autotheory that has recently emerged. At face value it reads as a strategy to hedge uncertainty, providing the personal terms and conditions to justify going out on a limb that one is not even sure of. On a deeper, historical reading, it is a practice initiated by Black feminists and queer artists since the 1970s in reclaiming everything not

allowed into the canon—the personal, emotions, senses, lived experience.[5] More cynically, it is the moment that Foucault's biopolitics[6] warned of, that even the subjective experience of the self would become performed under the guise of the internalised disciplining gaze. The personal is political, and now it has been monetised. If we are to reworld, or reword as it were, how can our post-design efforts be resistant to capitalist appropriation? Uhm might be read as an error, might be read as an opaque glitch.

24 "...As regards to this post...everything, uh, conversation post-human, post critical post-political, uh, post design. It does strike me that, on the one hand, it seems that we were still searching for what design in fact means or could entail when we try to see it, um, as, as, as, as opposed to its own Western tradition rooted in industrialization. Um, but somehow try to understand our belief systems and how problematic they are in terms of their racialized gendered, um, Eurocentric perspective. And, Um, that's, um..."

25 In the solutions-oriented paradigm of design, the glitch or problem is often the brief or starting point of the design process. What if instead we recognised these glitches as a refusal? Refusals that withhold time and attention from the tireless appropriating mechanism of modernity/coloniality; refusals of ever striving to be modern; refusals that advance more-than-modern ways of learning, being and designing for a still inarticulable and unconceived reality? Uhm is a refusal to be read, a refusal to be solved or designed away. Is post-design a refusal? It's worth remembering that post-modernism and post-colonialism are

not an end of modernism or colonialism, but rather a hyper accentuation of the multiplicities and seeming inescapability. A shifting of who's in power, if anything, and a solidification of structure. Then post-design is hardly redemptive, and perhaps we are already in post-design, if we consider how, when the solution-oriented design paradigm is challenged, design only seems to multiply and expand its omnipotence, from the world of design to the design of the world, from the word of design to the design of the word. On the other hand, perhaps because de-sign is already performed with the prefix of de-, meaning "not, do the opposite of, undo", post de-sign has a different unravelling of semiotics than post-design.

26 "...uh, post de-sign might be something of anticipation that it might be something that looks at what comes before design … the post de-sign practice might be situated in a pre-design phase or in a predesigned momentum…"

27 By de-signifying the temporality of progress, post de-sign could eschew design's "tradition of answering questions or bringing solutions or defining things, of making them readable, understandable". Instead, "what post de-sign revolves around is questions as an outcome, instead of answers. Instead of going from question to answer and then jumping to yet totally different questions in order to provide an answer, [post de-signers] might engage in a long-term process of going from question to question, which is a process of research." In a discipline no longer temporally defined in relation to solutions destined for market, post de-sign might be about expanding knowledge. Without the market as an index of value, what knowledge would be

de-signified. How would we know what we need to know? "Where design has had a tradition of being very grounded into all these event-based productions of jumping from topic to topic, having this grasshopper culture that you jump and fly from subject to subject, from project to project, going from question to question to question, there is this idea of longevity of temporality and therefore of commitment." The commitment to 'stay with the trouble' a la Donna Haraway is not involuntary, but considered and purposeful. Considered, purposeful and committed hesitance, uhming is just as active and productive as certainty when in a post de-sign temporality.

28 "...That's my dog. You can hear in the background, he likes to talk a lot..."

29 Speaking of Donna Haraway and the post-human call to expand our understanding of more-than-human agents, how do we spell the sound that the dog makes? How can we understand more-than-human voices? How can we understand even just one another's voices? The work of artist Alaa Abu Asad takes polylingual translation practice and invites friends to explore how subtle meaning differences of the same words, across different languages can be communicated. These discussions have also been translated through drawings, and the drawings and discussions have been translated into a book. With each translation, from agent to agent, from language to language, from medium to medium, something is lost and something is gained. Language is always an act of translation between experience and perception, between spoken and heard words. Language is a map, but we dare not lose sight of the territory,

especially when a new agent, 'the machine' and its data industrial complex, is prescribing a reading of the map that can sometimes take precedence over the territory and subjugate our interpretation of the map as incorrect. A post de-sign linguistic practice recognizes that the power of language lies in the constant negotiation of translation rather than the delegation of fixed positions. Every uhm is different. Uhm has no fixed position.

30 "...And I started to wonder what a hesitant designer would look like or feel like or how they would operate, um…"

31 A temporality of solutions and market-driven value also requires designers or curators to be expected to hold a position of certainty regarding what is presented, regardless of what knowledge might come to light. "What would it look like to acknowledge your vulnerability, acknowledge your uncertainty, um, what tools would you use and how would one operate?" Much like Herman Melville's Bartleby who "would prefer not to", could an uhm-position be not an absolute, but a mode of commitment, knowledge and vulnerability that in its opacity refuses capitalist appropriation by withholding time, attention and transmissibility? Could the post de-signer take an uhm-position of ongoing active embodied translation and re-translation that re-worlds through rewording across grammars, practices, mediums and agents?

32 "… the death maybe of, of design and, and if there's a death and what does it mean? Um, cause the way I'm trying to imagine it, or what popped up in my head is like a death, which is like more like a radical transformation,

which doesn't necessarily have to be, um, from one moment to another, but can happen also through transitioning. And what if this death would mean, um, dissolving like, uh, losing all these boundaries, all these definitions and, uh, categorical borders, which keeps one discipline together and separates one from the other. And, uh, and in this process or as a result of this, um, disappearing, uh, what other, um, maybe even invisible shape could happen, meaning like being a transmitter or like a membrane, which, um, instead of actively doing and undoing and restructuring and depatriarchising is just passively being there and present and connecting other existing moments and, and, um, entities together. And those are the ones who are acting. I dunno, I know it's a super, um, abstract, the explanation, but at this moment I cannot really, um, be more precise and, uh…"

33   Uhm is prophetic.[7] Uhm in its multiplicity and embodiment, is both resistant to denotation and resignification, is post de-signification. We can't quite pin down what it is we are saying into a neat lexicon of new words, but perhaps through uhm as a post de-sign linguistic practice there are ways in which we can begin to know differently. This is what transpired the collaborative uhming of Maxime Benvenuto, Fernand Bretillot, Ramón Jimenez Cardenas, Cecilia Casabona, Lara Chapman, Janfer Chung, Viktória Kaslik, Maxime Benvenuto, Sofia Irene Marmolejo Bijnsdorp, Tiiu Meiner and Josh Plough that took place in a Signal group in April 2021, and was translated by Nadine Botha, in conversation with Saskia van Stein.

34   Uhm is also a conclusion.

1 Olga Khazan. "Men Say ‚Uh' and Women Say ‚Um'." The Atlantic, 8 August 2014. https://www.theatlantic.com/health/archive/2014/08/men-say-uh-and-women-say-um/375729/

2 https://www.independent.co.uk/life-style/um-filler-words-discourse-markers-why-use-er-you-know-a7665721.html

3 Kathryn Yusoff. A Billion Black Anthropocenes or None. https://manifold.umn.edu/projects/a-billion-black-anthropocenes-or-none

4 "[Eve] Sedgwick once proposed that 'what it takes—all it takes—to make the description "queer" a true one is the impulse to use it in the first person,' and that anyone's use of 'queer about themselves means differently from their use of it about someone else'." (original emphasis) Maggie Nelson: 29. The Argonauts. Graywolf Press: Minneapolis, 2015.

5 Arianne Zwartjes, 'Autotheory as Rebellion: On Research, Embodiment, and Imagination in Creative Nonfiction', Michigan Quarterly Review Online. Available at: https://sites.lsa.umich.edu/mqr/2019/07/autotheory-as-rebellion-on-research-embodiment-and-imagination-in-creative-nonfiction/

6 Mitchell Dean and Daniel Zamora. (2021) 'Today, the self is the battlefield of politics. Blame Michel Foucault', The Guardian Online, 15 June. Available at: https://www.theguardian.com/commentisfree/2021/jun/15/michel-foucault-self-individual-politics

7 Federico Campagne, 2021, Prophetic culture, 1st edition, Bloomsbury Publishing, London.

wait
for it...

Alice Twemlow

Wait for it...

I am a blurter-outer. A just-in-time-think-as-I-speaker. A filler of pauses. An encouraging mmmm-er. I don't dare let a silence hang. What might crawl in?

> 'Silence has sometimes a remarkable power of showing itself as the disembodied soul of feeling wandering without its carcase...'
> Thomas Hardy, Far from the Madding Crowd, 1874

During the past year, many of us who work at the Royal Academy of Art The Hague (KABK) saw that our institution, like so many others of this era, is in urgent need of depatriarchalizing, decolonizing, reconstituting, and possibly even dismantling. The departure of our former director left a space that many of us hoped and imagined might be filled with a variant of collective leadership more representative of the academy's community of artists and designers, in all its neuro-gender-sexual-racial-cultural-weight-political-national-religious-class-disability-age-diversity.

In Zoom grids, open letters, Teams chat windows, Telegram groups, Instagram comment threads, on bathroom walls, and even in awkward IRL masked encounters in corridors, we discussed the matter. We conversed, shared views, deliberated, opinionated.

We suffered from meeting FOMO—even in a meeting, hearing the Teams' cry...—and sometimes tried to attend more than one at the same time. 'Sorry, wrong chat'. For most of the time, we were out of synch, our threads crossing, our video images glitching, freezing, multiplying, or disappearing; our privileges restored or revoked on the whim of a host, our presences were insubstantial, fractured. We canceled each other out. To speak became a game of chance as our words were transmitted in unpredictable rhythms: here, running into each other like cars in a pile up; there, stopping altogether—chopped up, blocked and muted.

> 'For centuries, stutterers seeking treatment had their mouths mutilated, their tongues cut into chunks, their palates scored like bread dough [...] Stutterers have had grass fibers burned on their skin, they have had knitting needles driven through their tongues, they have been forced to drink tonics composed of goat feces'.
> Jake Wolff, 'A Stutterer's Guide to Writing Fiction', 2019

We lost our connections. Very soon, I was tired out. I faltered. I doubted. And then, finally, I shut up.

> 'Geologists call a discontinuity in the deposition of sediment an unconformity. It's a physical representation of a gap in the geological record, a material sign of a break in time [...] The most famous is Hutton's Unconformity at Siccar Point near Edinburgh [...] with its uptilted and eroded gray wracke resting directly below the more horizontal layer of gently sloping red sandstone laid down sixty-five million years later, is both a seam and a rupture: a juxtaposition that reveals a cleft that can't be closed'.
> Hugh Raffles, The Book of Unconformities: Speculations on Lost Time, 2020

Around this time, curator Joannette van der Veer invited me to contribute to the 'unununimimimdeded-edesign' project, to consider the concept of the so-called stutter or halt in relation to art and design education, and current demands for unlearning and decentering the institutions of art and design education.

Stuttering **is a term used to describe a speech dysfluency where someone finds themselves involuntarily repeating a consonant or a syllable several times, prolonging a sound for a long time, or unable to get a particular word out, coming to a standst—**

My first thought was, Yes! the institution *is* stuttering, in the sense that it is repeating itself, that certain tenures and attitudes are prolonged beyond their use value, while alternatives are not even attempted or, worse, they are blocked.

My next thought was, No! the institution *needs* stuttering—and the way it forces a break, a pause, a hesitation, a rupture in the flow of words, in the multi-channel babble. KABK could use some of that.

> 'Obfuscation strategies represent creative ways to evade surveillance, protect privacy, improve security; as well as protest, contest, resist and sabotage technology. Obfuscation methods render data more ambiguous, difficult to exploit and interpret, less useful. They rely on the addition of gibberish, meaningless data; they pollute, add noise...'
> Jara Rocha, 'A Catalogue of Formats for Digital Discomfort', 2021

But that's because I was still...

> 'Yes, a situation can become interesting, [...] if it has been produced by a concrete learning process, in which the difficulties, the hesitations, the choices and errors are as much a part of the narrative as the successes and the conclusions arrived at'.
> Isabelle Stengers, Catastrophic Times: Resisting the Coming Barbarism, 2015

...learning. Or at least, I had forgotten what a tempting trap 'metaphoric thinking' can be. In her 1978 book *Illness as Metaphor*, Susan Sontag condemns the usage of illness for metaphoric purposes, yet, still, some of us often try to frame something difficult, like a speech dysfluency or an institutional crisis, in such analogous terms, in order to make it more comprehensible, more narratively cogent, more fitting to a familiar worldview.

Metaphors of flow, change, transparency and openness are appealing but they have been almost wholly co-opted by neoliberal creative industries and their techno-colonial regimes.

But even with metaphors of discontinuity, hesitation, disruption, and stoppage, we still run the risk of defaulting to normative assumptions. Moreover, trying to co-opt or instrumentalize stuttering for any kind of cause, be it political or creative, or to rebuild art and design education from its own ruins; is to recast a speech impairment in a positive light, to see what it has to offer, to give it generative agency—

— well, that's just a bit...

> 'There was no fluency anywhere.
> It was all stuttering.'
> Philip Roth, American Pastoral, 1997

Even in his rejection of semiotics-derived signification and metaphor, Gilles Deleuze's privileging of 'the writer who becomes a stutterer in language', for their ability to disrupt the smooth flow of normalizing discourses, puts him right back in the realm of metaphor. Especially when he goes further and personifies language itself as a stutterer. Language becomes so 'strained' at its extreme limit of disequilibrium, he posits, 'that it starts to stutter, or to murmur or stammer… then language in its entirety reaches the limit that marks its outside and makes it confront silence'.

> 'Th-Th-The, Th-Th-The, Th-Th… That's all, folks!'
> Porky Pig, 1935–

And when Simon O'Sullivan argues that what 'constitutes the ethico-aesthetic function of art' is the 'stuttering and stammering of existent materials and languages', I find myself wondering how the speech impairment feels about having to put its services to work for the noble cause of art.

Stuttering is not a choice, a tactic, an intervention, a literary style nor an artistic tool; it happens because of faulty signal transduction in the brain. And while many believe that it results from trauma or deprivation; it is usually inherited and untethered to psychology.

So when Joannette told me there was a stuttering typeface she was using for the 'unununimimimdedededesign' project, I was nervous. It sounded a lot like a visual metaphor.

Its designer, Lot Mars, experiences stuttering herself and wanted to make a typeface that would express how it feels bodily and emotionally for the stutterer and thereby give other people insight into the complexities of stuttering. She added extra pieces of punctuation, or accents, that litter the baseline like carcasses, physically taking up space with their awkward silent refusals of smooth communication. Through these devices, Mars wanted to draw attention to 'the duration of speaking and incorporate the concept of time into written writing'. I learned a lot spending time with this recalcitrant typeface.

Before the Stotts typeface was available, if a writer wanted to approximate silence on the page, they had to make do with the odds and ends in the typesetter's type tray. Paratextual elements such as ellipses and double dashes could be used to create suspense, to self-censor, to eloquently curtail speech or to reach out to the reader for help in completion of an idea.

In his novel, *The Life and Opinions of Tristram Shandy, Gentleman, 1759-1767*, Lawrence Sterne, disrupted the flow of the text with the insertion of white space (a blank page is offered to the reader for the purpose of composing their own description or portrait of Widow Wadman's beauty), and the obliteration of space (a black page 'mourns' the death of Yorick). Through these, and other typographical experiments Sterne brought attention to the texture of the page, to see if, despite written language's disabilities, silence could assert itself.

A few centuries later, in *A Primer for the Punctuation of Heart Disease*, a short story by the American author Jonathan Safran Foer, we find another typographic attempt to grasp the texture of silence. The narrator considers that his family has a whole alphabet of silences with which they (don't) communicate with one another. He proposes a new way of punctuating dialogue to denote all the varieties of unspoken import and puts this range of silence marks, 'willed' silence marks, 'insistent' question marks, and 'should-have' brackets, into action at the end of the story in a heart-rending telephone conversation between a son and father with heart disease:

> "Are you hearing static?"
> "{I'm crying into the phone}."
> "Jonathan?"
> "silence mark"
> "Jonathan?"
> "willed silence mark"
> "{A child's sadness is a parent's sadness.}"
> "{A parent's sadness is a child's sadness.}"
> "I'm probably just tired."
>
> Jonathan Safran Foer, 'A Primer for the Punctuation of Heart Disease', 2002

According to Ellen Samuels in 'Six Ways of Looking at Crip Time', disability has the 'power to extract us from linear, progressive time with its normative life stages and cast us into a wormhole of backward and forward acceleration, jerky stops and starts, tedious intervals and abrupt endings'.

> That sounds tiring. But it's a good thing, right?

The Social Model of Disability proposes that social structures and attitudes define disability, rather than people's impairments. It therefore carries the implication that the physical, attitudinal, communicative and social environment must change to enable people living with impairments to participate in society on an equal basis with others. Or, as Johanna Hedva puts it, 'You don't need to be fixed, my queens. It's the world that needs to be fixed'.

> Jake is speaking…

> > 'But now I recognise the barrier, I can relax, I can even ask you, simply and assertively, to listen to what I am saying. In this way I can carve out a place to be dysfluent and less disabled'.
> > Jake Wolff, 'A Stutterer's Guide to Writing Fiction', 2019

So just as we are—I am—on the brink of newly learned speech, instead, let us—let me—practice waiting, and learn to listen.

> ~~Alice is typing…~~

Let's dwell a while longer in that ellipsis of careful omission, and willed silence, and submit to, or celebrate, the double dash of dysfluency. Let's hold the speech space for those who have had to go against the flow, feel the friction, and whose voices have been blocked. It's okay; all the words that are needed will come along. In time.

the design exit: don't look behind!

Imad Gebrayel

The Design Exit: Don't Look Behind!

hesitations of a field in ⟶turn and ⟶turmoil

The Design Exit is a project that negotiates repositioning design outside of the art-school system (within a European-context), and discusses the overdue critical turn in design education as a form of alter-reality.

A critical turn took place in the early 1970s among scholars in the humanities and social sciences to make cultures, criticality, decoloniality and plural relations the foci of contemporary debates; whilst also demonstrating a shift in emphasis toward meaning, and away from a positivist epistemology.[1] Design is only 50 years late to this debate. The field is in need of a shift into a new era outside of the art academy, away from solutionism and design-positivism.[2]

The Design Exit was launched as a series of digital round-tables for the months of September, October, and November 2020 hosted by Imad Gebrayel with guest participants: Ahmed Ansari, Chris Lee, Eva Gonçalves, Maya Ober, Nadine Rotem, Nina Paim, Sara Kaaman, Sérgio Miguel Magalhães and Zoy Anastassakis. The aim was to start an active, open-ended debate about design, design education and disciplinary boundaries.

This essay threads auto-ethnographic passages with excerpts from the series, where fragmentation and messiness become intentional carriers of open-ended questions and reflections. Contrary to popular belief, this essay does not provide solutions. I hereby share provocative hesitations and self-reflexive thoughts on my own positionality in liminal[3] spaces between design academia and anthropology. While complicit in disseminating (and resisting) colonial academic structures through teaching and studying in colonial institutions, I believe in using my (precarious) position to entice counter-disciplinary thinking, self-critical knowledge production and unions. I believe in unions.

an auto-ethnographic vignette

I landed in the Netherlands after 3 years of hard work in graphic design, saving every coin to escape a country drenched in trauma. While struggling with my mediocre biking skills, I reached the masters institute, situated in an old monastery surrounded by tall trees and corn fields. It was an archetypal European art-school housing numerous artistic disciplines including design. I had to readjust to many things; my skin color, body hair, Dutch cheese sandwiches and the realities I was expected to invest in (quite literally). The art-school in most European contexts ranks below the university system, yet both are equally exclusive. I realized that the road would be bumpy and that I had to improve my biking skills.

critical, ~~but make a chair~~

While looking for higher design education, prospective students (often with too much at stake) walk a dangerous minefield, continuously misled by programs trying to tick multiple boxes but rarely delivering on their promises.

I experienced the latter first-hand in 2014 when fields like social, service and interaction design were emerging and I had to closely examine graduation projects, seek insider information through alumni, and connect the dots: a well-known program on social design that often produced chairs, products and art installations, with parachute-trips to Africa seemed tempting to many, but highly alarming to me.

I currently see this occurrence happening again with friends and colleagues as they seek opportunities to leave Lebanon after the total collapse of the political and economic system. **A design program is sometimes a way out, an unclaimed, unlabeled, unofficial asylum- seeking process for individuals struggling with different forms of oppression, wanting an exit-route that isn't necessarily terminal.**

"The programs I found myself attracted to were the ones that used the correct jargon for my profile [...] but I ended up very confused as a lot of them sold big ideas but failed to get into the specifics, so I either would not spot the differences or I would believe the big promises only to find out later, when I received further documents from admission, that the program or the university were not what they claim to be on their website"
Nermine, Lebanon.

"Programs are always advertising their market value using terms like "innovative" and "strategic" while highlighting the career opportunities one might land. I never got a detailed explanation of the curriculum as they only listed course-titles. Many of my peers were asking for more details to pick a module but we never received it until the day of the introductory class. That was too late, we had registered already'.
Josiane, Lebanon.

Such experiences barely scratch the surface of the performative criticality design academia uses to attract foreign student investments. This dynamic mirrors the white-saviorism often embedded in design schools claiming socially-engaged agendas: "*I want to take students to Beirut, they need us there*", stated a program-coordinator during a recent exchange.

Design criticality is not a linear process that starts with good intentions and ends with a chair, an infographic or even a re-invented ramp. Art-schools housing critical design programs lack a basic infrastructure allowing for critical thinking, as well as adequate exposure to theoretical frameworks, political discussions and access to different forms

of research. Curating a selection of Metahaven publications is nothing but lacking.

Knowledge is buildable; design students operating within the bubble of their remote Harry-Potter campuses need to access other institutions, events, collaborations, discussions, dissertations, libraries and communities. Designers have the potential to advance a pre-existing body of research but they are often positioned in a vacuum.

I spent 2 years trouble-making. My master's degree was a painful journey of resistance where I had to fight for a focus on research and wanted to produce a qualitative thesis on colonial visual representation, but faced the main systemic hurdle: accreditation. "You cannot change the assessment criteria for graduation. A theoretical thesis is not enough and a design project is indispensable", stated the coordinators. Such barriers are systemic structures designed and sustained by a teaching body seeking a ticket to the hype-train without wanting to deal with any form of accountable change. Speed-boarding, stress-free.

‎‐boarding ‎the hype-‎train

Design, a field conceived by—and flourishing through—capitalism, often seeks volatile renditions of capital, fusing selective politics within academic curricula and mediating EngagementTM.

EngagementTM, an imaginary design brand that gained a high level of visibility in recent years through the rise of social media platforms, aimed at resurrecting a field from the ashes of its own obsoleteness. Design programs historically celebrating the "creative (European male) genius" moved from an early focus on "function, value and quality", to one of "criticality". For example, a quick look at design master's programs in the Netherlands shows a massive emergence of disciplines like social design, critical studies, visual cultures, situated design, geo- design, contextual design and ecology futures, to name but a few. Master's programs keep on rebranding on a yearly basis in the hopes of attracting investors (foreign students) to the business model of European design education and its gated art-school system.

Let me restate that I am not arguing against design programs experimenting with their own positioning or seeking to advance their political content. In fact I am all for open access to criticality and for mainstreaming theoretical debates even at the risk of emptying them from their "presumed" exclusive value. Recent debates on decolonization gained momentum in design education, and decolonial scholars raised valid concerns over the volatile engagement of design with decolonization and the dangers of using such frameworks as thematic topics or even as metaphors[4] favoring settler futures. With such concerns in mind, I still stand in favor of mainstreaming knowledge processes for they were never meant to live in exclusive academic structures.

I recently joined a call hosted by a coordinator at a German art school about decolonization and design. The call soon revealed the school's intentions to curate a conference to fund a research project where they sought visiting lecturers from Africa (the whole continent), China, and India, and to practice "non-hegemonic teaching", a term coined by the coordinator at that very moment. The coordinator, claiming the majority of speaking time, refused structural change at the level of the curriculum: "I tried doing that before, the professors will not agree". Another invited educator suggested offering half of her already-precarious lectureship to a woman with less access. She sees herself as a facilitator who can afford sharing.

This is what happens in design academia, a solutionist, white-saviorist approach to intersectional struggles. A continuous reassertion of power, privilege and a constant reminder of the borders one cannot cross. Our colored, queer bodies are often seen as good display windows for EngagementTM but never as active agents of—unsettling—structural change.

orders, =borders and hoarders

Moving beyond the notion of the "broken"[5] system, I suggest an approach meeting the social sciences, anthro-pology to be exact. Somewhere in a liminal space where design students are taught qualitative and quantitative research methods and can therefore access different disciplines. I am not promoting anthropology as a solution (I'm anti-solutionism, remember?) but as a potential ground for para-siting,[6] for co-laboration[7] and multimodality[8] within the broken, colonial university system. I am all for abolishing disciplines to begin with (as suggested by Nina Paim during an informal conversation at Südblock, Berlin), but until then, I suggest occupying space from "without" (the art-school).

I am calling for leaving the art-school campus behind, for it to dwell in its own mysticism, its constant pursuit of the contemporary, and its stigma of the misunderstood creative genius, and focus on a space where designers are in exchange with historians, scientists, data analysts, journalists, and anthropologists. Where designers work in/with the field rather than at it. In engaging with such ethnographic approaches, designers are not expected to reproduce ethnography's colonial history, nor its exclusive focus instead on the problem, but rather address problems collaboratively and systemically, as the verve for design's approach to solving problems can often stand in the way of addressing the complex systems that create the problem in the first place.[9]

a housing crisis or structural decay?

During *The Design Exit* conversations, we discussed the tight grid of hesitations when negotiating a complete repositioning of design programs and curricula. A very subjective selection of such discussions reveals two main issues I will reformulate as "present bodies" and "absent histories". The entanglements of the bodies blocking access and those resisting intensify design's ontological turn and move the positioning debate from a housing crisis (inside/outside of the art-school) into structural impossibilities: the European art-school—as we know it—is in fact no longer habitable.

present bodies:

The design turn, and its accompanying hesitations as labeled in this essay, are not only facing structural challenges in finding positioning within the academy, the vocational schools or the applied science universities in Europe, but are also experiencing a highly problematic crisis of the bodies occupying their spaces. Maya Ober invites us to look into the people forming the teaching bodies: "they come from a very narrow understanding of what a design practice is. [...] this kind of design production monopolizes education and does not allow for more theory or research-based practices". Parallel to the strong division between different academic classifications of higher education models, Ober discusses the structural barriers set by the people creating curricula, including what they value and what they do not, in favor of studies that feed the capitalist needs of the labour market.

Nina Paim, discussing her own experience with experimental positionings of design (currently researching within the Laboratory of Design and Anthropology LaDA), student unions and on- campus activism at ESDI-Brazil, seconds Ober's opinion, marking a direct correlation between the bodies that

Imad Gebrayel

occupy all the important decision-making processes, and curricula-forming positions within the schools and the demographics they represent.

ab-sent histories

The question of bodies, identifications and their entanglements with space-time[10] reveals a deeper need for the reconstruction of field-specific histories before addressing the positioning turmoil. Is design a field with no theory, or is design-specific theory (not the one we appropriate from other disciplines) concealed in favour of material production?

Ahmed Ansari reveals another concern via the main question of *The Design Exit*, as he recaps different approaches to the debate on design affiliations with the social, natural or artificial sciences, the arts and humanities, and totally autonomous positionings. Ansari discusses Nigel Cross's[11] and Richard Buchanan's[12] talk about a third culture. Central to hesitations around positioning comes a knowledge gap in design education, according to Ansari: "We do not teach this stuff right. Very rarely". He further refers to the ontological turn in advocating for developing a sense of one's own discipline's history and a critical relation to it: "They are kind of working from recreating the wheel; this refers to the constant need therefore to not only "rediscover" discourses that are ages old, but a general tendency to bring in and immediately instrumentalize extra-disciplinary knowledge without any real understanding of what the histories behind that knowledge are too".[13]

Connecting bodies and histories becomes a crucial aspect of the hesitations discussed in this essay; the bodies and histories of those who once asserted imperialism through academia, those who sustain their hegemonic presence through exclusive structures, texts and spaces, and those who resist, for it is only with those who resist that design can find new figurations.[14]

conclusion

Throughout this essay, I discussed a provocation advocating for design to exit the art-school system in the European context. Drenched in excessive production, performative criticality, gatekeeping and a continuous appropriation of histories and knowledges, design programs need to account for an overdue turn. While acknowledging that academia cannot effectively challenge the coloniality of power for it is intrinsically "designed" to sustain it,[15] I believe that designers should have better access to scientific research, within and outside the art academy, in tight dialogue with different sites and disciplines.
For subverting, advancing or even abolishing a decaying field cannot be made a solo endeavour: it takes a group to Dabke.[16]

1 Also referred to as "positivism", referring to the school of research thought that sees observable evidence as the only form of defensible scientific finding. Positivist epistemology, therefore, assumes that only "facts" derived from the scientific method can make legitimate knowledge claims. It also assumes the researcher is separate from, and not affecting the outcomes of research. "What Is Positivist Epistemology," IGI Global, accessed May 12, 2021, https:// www.igi-global.com/dictionary/positivist-epistemology/23062.

2 A common jargon promoting design as a problem-solving discipline, amplified by subfields like design thinking and innovation labs. Such understandings of design—when intersecting with Othered communities—create volatile, void and apolitical outcomes favouring design (and designers) over accountable, sustainable engagement.

3 A position that is "ambiguous, neither here nor there, betwixt and between all fixed points of classification" (Turner 1974:232). I advocate for understanding *liminality* through the lens of black feminist authors developing the concept towards *double-liminality*: FRANCES E. MASCIA-LEES, PATRICIA SHARPE, and COLLEEN B. COHEN, "Double Liminality and the Black Woman Writer." American Behavioral Scientist 31, no. 1 (1987): pp. 101-114. https:// doi.org/10.1177/000276487031001007.

4 Eve Tuck and K. Wayne Yang. "Decolonization is not a metaphor," *Decolonization: Indigeneity, education & society* vol. 1, no. 1 (2012): 1-40.

5 Tony Fry, "Design Education in a Broken World," The Studio at the Edge of the World, http://www.thestudioattheedgeoftheworld.com/uploads/4/7/4/0/47403357/fry-designeducation.pdf

6 Refers to collaboration between multiple sites of knowledge: a type of field situation that neither takes the shape of horizontal relations nor implies the erasure of (disciplinary) differences. On the contrary, the para-sitical collaboration […] is often brought into existence against a background of disciplinary frictions, differing knowledges, epistemic diversity and social misunderstandings. Adolfo Estalella and Tomás Sánchez Criado, eds., *Experimental Collaboration: Ethnography Through Fieldwork Devices* (S.l.: Berghahn Books, 2018).

7 Co-laborative: joint epistemic work aimed at producing disciplinary reflexivities, not interdisciplinary shared outcomes. Jörg Niewöhner, "Co-laborative anthropology: Crafting Reflexivities Experimentally." In "Ethnologinen tulkinta ja analyysi. Kohti avoimempaa tutkimusprosessia, eds. Jukka Jouhki and Tytti Steel (Helsinki: Ethnos, 2016) 81-125. Originally published in Finnish, accessed online. https://edoc.hu-berlin.de/bitstream/handle/18452/19241/Niewoehner2016-Co-laborative-anthropology.pdf?sequence=1&isAllowed=y

8 Multimodality and its (occasional) double, multi-sensoriality, as terms that have recently been utilised in anthropology for thinking about, and with the media ecologies—that is, the multiple media(tions)—in which we live. MULTIMODAL ANTHROPOLOGIES, Special Series: Multimodal Inventions. Introduction: Multimodal Anthropology and the Politics of Invention. Ethiraj Gabriel Dattatreyan and Isaac Marrero-Guillamón.

9 Elizabeth Chin (2016): Collaboration: Deviation.

10 Doreen Massey 1999

11 Nigel Cross suggests design as a discipline, rather than design as a science: "this discipline seeks to develop domain-independent approaches to theory and research in design. The underlying axiom of this discipline is that there are forms of knowledge peculiar to the awareness and ability of a designer, independent of the different professional domains of design practice". (Michel, 2007)

12 Nigel Cross suggests design as a discipline, rather than design as a science: "this discipline seeks to develop domain-independent approaches to theory and research in design. The underlying axiom of this discipline is that there are forms of knowledge peculiar to the awareness and ability of a designer, independent of the different professional domains of design practice". (Michel, 2007)

13 Ansari sees the central problem in design pedagogy being the conservatory as the principal site of training for designers, with very few variations within that model; modern conservatories still rely on artificial and debunked distinctions between theory, research and practice, and rarely hire experts that have non-design backgrounds. […] Furthermore, he thinks of design as its own thing, a third culture: "I don't think having it classified as a social science is going to do designers any favors, just as being part of the "arts" or "sciences" doesn't help either. I don't think that constantly having to justify our research to sociologists, anthropologists and economists etc. is going to be very useful, especially given how universities tend to operate".

14 Figurations are dynamic networks of people bonded through mutual dependencies over space and time or, in Norbert Elias's own words, "a structure of mutually orientated and dependent people... the network of interdependencies formed by individuals" (Elias, 2000, p. 482).

15 Inspired by *"The Master's Tools Will Never Dismantle the Master's House"* by Black lesbian feminist writer and activist Audre Lorde. Lorde, Audre. *"The Master's Tools Will Never Dismantle the Master's House." 1984. Sister Outsider: Essays and Speeches. Ed. Berkeley, CA: Crossing Press. 110-114. 2007. Print.*

16 A folk dance native to the region, including Palestine, Lebanon, Syria, Iraq and Jordan. Dabke combines circle dance and group line dancing and is widely performed at weddings and other joyous occasions.

affective classroom: on choosing life, vulnerability and weakness in design education.

Maya Ober
(depatriarchise design)

Affective classroom: on choosing life, vulnerability and weakness in design education

Discourses around design education mainly focus on content, references, canon, assignments and evaluations; yet, we give little attention to the intimate, affective relations between teachers and students. These intimate everyday practices evoke a myriad of feelings from love and happiness to shame and hate.

design is not for the weak

Students in a classroom hang out their sketches which have been meticulously drawn with Pantone markers and placed on cardboard or polyurethane mockups on shattered podiums. Since there are not enough displays for everyone, we improvise by using ugly grey plastic chairs back from the 90s' as an exhibiting space. The professor enters, and we begin our weekly routine. Each person stands up, shortly presents what they were working on, and the critique starts. First, the fellow students would speak, giving their feedback ranging from helpful technical tips on materials and technologies to sarcastic comments meant to ridicule the person speaking. Finally, the professor takes a turn to talk; he takes a mockup in his hand, the same mockup you would sand until late in the night, getting your whole body covered in a cancerogenic polyurethane dust, the one you would wait tables in two different restaurants to be able to pay for. Almost as if it was nothing, something utterly devoid of any value, he throws it into the rubbish bin or drops it onto the floor. In the end, he knows, and he marks it worthless. He would also mention how you and two-thirds of your class are not suited for industrial design. A week after, the whole year would wear newly designed stickers: "Me too. I am not suited for industrial design". Humour, resourcefulness, and graphic design would become our resistance.

Many students, mostly female, would cry during these critiques. The feelings of public humiliation, shame, and hate mixed with one another. Each ruthlessly criticized project invoked almost physical pain as if it was a limb, an extension of your body and a direct connection to your soul. They were not evaluating your work, instead they were evaluating you as a designer. You are worth what your design is worth. So following this logic, if your design is 'worthless', then you are 'worthless' too. If your design is not "good enough", you are thus judged useless for a design school.

> "It is not worth you staying"
> "It is a waste of time."
> "Find another profession, something you would be useful for."
> "You are not suited for design."

This is a particular scene that would repeat itself time and again during my undergraduate studies, one that, in the end, I normalized to the extent that it became almost an exclusive model of design pedagogy and affective relations.

But how does being marked as 'worthless', and hence 'useless' *affect* you as a student? What does it *do* to you? Feminist theorist Sara Ahmed in her book "What's the use? On the uses of use", writes about how *use* is a technique to fulfill one's potential thoroughly, so "nothing is left idle" (2019, p. 103). This way, by being deemed useless, you are not worthy of existing within the educational machine. You slow it down; you are a burden, you decrease the efficiency. So not only is your design useless, and you are useless, but because your design performance is useless you then affect everyone else, you are spreading the "uselessness". You are weak; therefore you should cease to exist. You should leave. Design is not for the weak. Neither is a design school.

This functionalist, results-oriented underpinning of design "education" calls for our attention. If you are judged useless, it means that you failed your *training*. You are not able to *perform*, to *follow* the steps of a procedure instilled in you. Maybe your 3D modeling skills are not as proficient, your sketches don't conform to the marker rendering beauty standards, your CAD plans are quirky, or your concept doesn't fit the rigid disciplinary boundaries of 'proper' industrial design.

I purposefully use the term 'training', as the described framework constitutes, in my opinion, a 'design training' rather than design education. Here, I draw on the work of anthropologist Tim Ingold. He writes about education as a practice of "correspondence with this world" rather than a practice of instilling "awareness of the world around us" (Ingold, 2013, p. 28). If we *attend to the world*, echoing Ingold, we continuously expose ourselves to different viewpoints; we are constantly "out-of-position". So we are weak, vulnerable, and attentive "to respond to a reality the world presents to us" (Ingold, 2013, p. 34). This education is about care and being in the world with others, out of the comfort zone of desired knowledge, reason and pre-established ways of designing. Instead of being molded into a polished, brilliant cube, we expose ourselves, we are dis-oriented, we focus on life. Focusing on life, means not only living in the current moment, rather as Ingold proposes, it lets every moment become a new beginning. (Ingold, 2013)

_the out_cast _body

Entering the classroom, we begin imagining and shaping futures. The future is particularly important in design, as proposed by Colombian anthropologist Arturo Escobar, as a "powerful ontological tool capable of transforming the social and cultural reality, and modeling human experience, subjectivity and lifestyle, and environment and social events" (Escobar, 2018, p. 133). Design can be understood as a process of world-making. We design the environment and what we have designed is designing us in turn.

But what worlds are we making in the classroom? Black feminist scholar bell hooks points out in her essay "Eros, Eroticism and the pedagogical process" (1993) that there is a split between body and mind once we enter the classroom. Our bodies are erased in the design educational space; they don't exist, though they *do* exist. Following europatriarchal logic, the classroom is the space of reason, not emotions, affects, and corporalities. However, as described by Chicana feminist author Gloria Anzaldua, "those who are pushed out of the tribe for being different are likely to become more sensitized [...] — the females, the homosexuals of all races, the dark skinned, the outcast, the persecuted, the marginalized, the foreign." (1985, p. 38).

The condition of being an "outcast", which is often 'visible' through the culturally and socially constructed perception of the body, in a way, predestines us to work against hegemonic structures, creating new futures *now*. The way you speak, your accent, your pregnant belly, your skin color, how you move, your look, how you don't conform to the gender binary, your 'difference' makes you hyper-visible in the classroom. On the other hand, we are expected to suppress our bodies, disregard and ignore them, while at the same time, we are coming together and joining ourselves in one space across our differences.

I am interested in these instances of us being together and how our corporeality plays a role in design education. Whenever I talk to the students, my strong, foreign accent in German resonates through the walls. It is never 'neutral'. I am always visible through my voice. This feeling of hypervisibility amplified during my pregnancy. I tried so hard to be just 'the reason' in the classroom, to make my body disappear. However, it took over me. And when you are pregnant, you are foremostly perceived through the lens of your difference. Your pregnant body doesn't belong to the public, to the academia, but it is nevertheless in the room. The fetus moves and kicks, your feet are swollen, you can't bend, your back hurts, your breasts sometimes surprisingly leek, exactly when you are wearing a bright shirt and talking to a student. You are not in "control"; you're not just a teacher; you are a pregnant, foreign teacher. You are also an activist engaged in anti-discriminatory feminist work. The work is time-consuming and kills the joys of so many, echoing Sara Ahmed.

However, during this pregnancy, I tried hard to disconnect my growing belly and body from my educational practice. In hindsight, it was a subconscious strategy of resisting highly homogenous structures and spaces in which any "difference" stands out. Euro-patriarchal, modernity-driven logic that dominates design education circumscribes racialized, gendered, non-abled bodies through the lens of their 'difference,' often creating spaces in which "outcasts" prefer to disappear, rather than be constantly addressed and reduced to their difference. When I was pregnant, I wanted to disappear.

But there is a place for new beginnings, for a long overdue design education *otherwise*. Fostering educational practices, as proposed by design researcher and educator Danah Abdulla, opens possibilities towards design *otherwise*, that is critical, situated, reflexive, and socially transformative (Abdulla, 2018). After nine months of trying to disappear, of ignoring my body, of crying secretly in the bathroom—as crying in public in front of my peers or students could be perceived as weakness–the last thing I wanted in a heteropatriarchal society was to be considered weak, vulnerable. I had to be strong, to work, perform, despite pregnancy, despite hurdles, despite wanting only to lay down and do nothing. I felt that only by working as if it wasn't there, I could guarantee myself not being addressed or perceived as a pregnant person, or further, as a parent. Since I couldn't eradicate my accent, though I have tried, and

I couldn't change my gender identity; I could at least try ignoring pregnancy or parenting. Time has shown that it didn't work, and the patriarchy would strike time after time, regardless of how much I tried to resist it. Even though I worked 'as if' I wasn't pregnant, 'as if' I wasn't hurting from congested breast tissue, 'as if' I wasn't exhausted after an insomniac night. 'As if' became a form of resistance.

the pandemic-epilogue

Due to the COVID-19 pandemic, which forced us to blur even further the lines between the public and the domestic sphere, I have started to bring motherhood into the virtual classroom with me. My kid would appear on the screen as she curiously climbed my lap to see with whom I was talking with. I stopped muting my microphone when she would scream or cry from the living room, and I would hold her with me when she wanted. Her body became present. Multiple feminists activists who vulnerably exposed themselves in numerous online lectures, workshops and talks opened the door for me, to resist the "neutral" hegemonic, often white and male-dominated educational space, by bringing not only my baby in, but also the extreme exhaustion, the constant illness, the pain of engorged breast and the leeking, the fear, the frustration of the passed deadlines. All the different emotions that accompanied me during my first years as a parent.

Recently, I listened to an online lecture by Brazilian curator, writer, researcher, heiress griot, and shaman, Keyna Eleison. She speaks about how motherhood is about choosing life. This thought resonated with me because by choosing life, we choose being together, we choose community, we choose an education that embraces life and differences, education that cares, and through which we are attuned to each other. By becoming weak and vulnerable, I expose myself in this text and in the everyday, in every class, choosing life and the future now.

Works cited

Ahmed, Sara. *What's the Use?*. Durham: Duke University Press, 2019.

Ingold, Tim. *Making: Anthropology, Archaeology, Art and Architecture*. London: New York: Routledge, 2013.

Escobar, Arturo. *Designs for the Pluriverse*. Durham: Duke University Press, 2018.

hooks, bell, 1993. 'Eros, Eroticism and the pedagogical process', Cultural Studies, 7:1, 58-63.

Anzaldúa, Gloria. *Borderlands / La Frontera: The New Mestiza*. San Francisco: aunt lute books, 1987.

Abdulla, D., Prado de O. Martins, L. and Schultz, T., 2018. 'Decolonising Design Education: Ontologies, Strategies, Urgencies'. In: J. Lindgren, ed. *Extra-Curricular*. Eindhoven: Onomatopee.pp.76–91.

reclaiming the unclaimed

a conversation between
Belle Phromchanya,
Darunee Terdtoontaveedej
and Joannette van der Veer

Reclaiming the unclaimed

JV   Joannette van der Veer
BP   Belle Phromchanya
DT   Darunee Terdtoontaveedej

JV   I thought it would be nice to start our conversation with you sharing a little bit about your background and practice, what do you think?

BP   Yes, so I studied graphic design back in Thailand. And then I decided to move to The Netherlands to study at the Sandberg Design Department in Amsterdam. I think the Sandberg was the place where I got to explore the world of design beyond the typical graphic design understanding, or, what I understood it to be. The understanding I had of graphic design was that it was mainly about designing identities for print or web communications, yet even back then I already had an interest in socially related subjects. So, my work leaned towards that kind of content, like the political movements that were happening in Thailand back in 2010 for instance. When I came to the Sandberg, I felt the field of (graphic) design to be much more open and that there were a lot more possibilities in terms of what design can be. I started making small films that would allow me to include elements such as voice, atmosphere, or the environment; elements that were important in presenting the things and topics I was working on. Elements I could not just then turn into an information graphic, for example.

JV   So, in a way, the graphic design tools were too limited for you?

BP   Yes, at a certain point it became too limited. Especially when I started working with subjects in relation to people.

JV   And how about you, Darunee?

DT   Well, I started off with studying architecture, actually, ten years ago in London at Central Saint Martins. But towards the end of my studies, I realised that I wasn't really interested in building buildings, but instead I was more interested in the ideas behind architecture. The knowledge-production aspect of architecture, exhibition-making for example. So I got involved with curating, and did an internship with the curators of the Lisbon Architecture Triennale in 2012/13. Afterwards, I went back to Thailand and dabbled into all kinds of different jobs, before ending up working for an architecture and design magazine publisher as a writer. And then, at some point, I got really bored with design and architecture in Bangkok because I thought it was very limited. And so I decided to come to The Netherlands and study Contextual Design at a Masters level at Design Academy Eindhoven. At that time, the Contextual Design department was headed by Louise Schouwenberg and I always felt like her ideas about design were contradicting each other. On the one hand she was questioning it, writing manifestos about why we should not make more things. Yet, on the other hand, she was head of a department that says it's mostly research-based, however a lot of people graduated with a piece of furniture. I felt like a lot of my issues and questions could not be addressed by just simply making an object. So I was not really happy with my studies. However, both my bachelor and master experiences allowed me to question the practice and ultimately made me realise that I don't want to be a designer. During my studies, I was interested in the idea of the home, domestication and identification with spaces and places, as well as the selves, but then of course all the surrounding questions could not be answered by design only, so I went on a journey of professional exploration after graduating After a while, I discovered that there is such a thing as film festival making and programming, so I started to work in film from there. In a way, it was very similar to curating.

un-settling relationship

JV   Belle, you mention that the subjects you deal with in your work are rooted in the unsettling relationship between yourself and the globalized society. Could you expand on why you consider this relationship to be unsettling?

BP   It goes back to when I moved to The Netherlands to study. I actually did not plan on staying here, yet I have now been living in The Netherlands for almost 10 years. Like I already mentioned before, the kind of work that I make here is rather different from what I was making in Thailand. Once I started to live abroad, there were certain things that pushed me towards the questioning of my own position in this particular part of the world. To study abroad is something you generally want to pursue and if you have the resources to do so, then it's like: "let's go abroad, see the world, and bring something back home". But then, I also enjoyed the energy of the design scene, the knowledge, and the people I met along the way while living here. At the same time, I am not sure if I belong to this location. These were the kind of things that were not only happening with me, but probably with everyone who decides to move and live in a place that they are not born in. There are certain parts of the new location, or city, or culture, or environment that you are attracted to, while at the same time—living in the globalised world—it is also hard for me to kind of leave everything behind. When I open up my computer, I still see news from Thailand in real time, and I am able to speak to my family and friends there anytime I wish to. It's like I'm not there in person, but my beliefs and my connection to the country are still in place. That is kind of conflicting as well. I notice this kind of conflict within others who live in diaspora communities and displacement and have produced projects such as 'Whether It Is Art or Not' and 'Capital of Mae La', that discuss the world of the outsiders. This kind of alienating notion is something I have always been interested in exploring.

> DT As Belle is saying about this unsettling relationship, I think we all have that. We all have a love-hate relationship with the place that we're in. The grass is always greener on the other side and so now we're here having something to complain about, but when we go to the other side we will also have something to complain about there. Before coming to The Netherlands I naively thought that this is a very open country. It is, after all, the first country that legalised gay marriage, allows marijuana, sex work, and all that. So, I think, they must be very open. And then I came here and I think I have experienced the worst racism I had ever experienced in my entire life living abroad. And so then there's a lot of cognitive dissonance. I noticed that the Dutch society is tolerant—tolerance is not the same as acceptance, so this means that they might not accept different customs, but they just put up with it. After being in the international bubble that is the Design Academy, I decided to move to Rotterdam. I did not

really know where to start or how I could get to know more Dutch people, so I started a project called "Neitherlands": a photography project with an interview element where I look for different Dutch people and I interview them about what it means to be Dutch. Most of the people I interviewed were not, say, Dutch Dutch. They were either born here or they immigrated here, but were not really seen as full Dutch citizens. So, still, perceived as kind of foreign, even though they speak perfect Dutch, and they cannot speak their mother tongue (anymore). So that was something I was always interested in, this kind of identity not matching what is expected. Or this notion of national identity being picked apart and destroyed, because I don't think there's such a thing as national identity anymore. But being 'foreign' also gives you special skills. Because you need to know how to survive in an environment that can be hostile. I know many people who have 'multiple personalities'—I think in English you call it code-switching, when you speak in a certain way to a certain group of people in order to make them feel like you're one of them. And then when you move to another social group, then perhaps you might also need to blend in, so you're basically a chameleon. I think that's a special skill, and I totally embrace that.

JV   **Like a skill of adaptation?**

DT   **A survival skill.**

JV   **Isn't that a sad thing?**

DT I mean, it's sad that you have to keep adapting to fit in somewhere. But adaptation is a basic instinct, it's very important everyone learns to adapt because the world keeps changing. You cannot just stay static—that's not possible. On the one hand it's sad, on the other it's necessary. Obviously, it would be nice if people could be their authentic selves and still be respected and loved and accepted in our very multifaceted society, but...

BP But do we even know what our authentic self is? I mean we switch to so many versions of ourselves, on and off... I don't even know if myself in The Netherlands, or myself in Thailand is the more authentic one. Or me being with my parents, or me being together with students, which of those is more authentic. So maybe we can think of this switching also as something to celebrate. That we have a choice to be able to change according to whatever it is we want to change to, and no one would even know—even yourself—which version is real.

JV True... And then, at some point, the two of you met and you founded Non Native Native. How did you actually meet?

DT After graduating from Design Academy I didn't really know what to do with myself. Also, I didn't really know what to do regarding my visa. Because eventually it would expire and then I would need to find a way to extend it. In The Netherlands there's a scheme called the artist visa; do you know that?

JV Yes, I do... I have been involved in some letters of recommendation.

DT Exactly!!! Recommendation, confirmation of whatever exhibitions and projects, something to prove that you are culturally valuable to The Netherlands. And, at that point, most of the people around me graduated with a piece, or set of furniture. Or objects, or sculptures, whatever. So they all found a way to be represented by galleries or at least had something tangible to sell, you know? I graduated with a couple of posters and a text that I wasn't entirely happy with, so I wasn't convinced enough to sell it somehow. I was talking to my friend, a common friend of ours, telling her that I didn't know what to do and that I was really worried about my situation. And then this friend was like "ah yeah, I know someone who might be similar to you, she just got her visa approved so maybe the two of you should talk". And then that's how we met.

BP Yes, we talked about the visa and also about work. She also explained to me about the Neitherlands project, and the fact that we are both Thai, so we also kind of clicked, in the sense that we can talk about social and political situations as well as random stuff in Thai. We became good friends. Before we initiated Non Native Native, I was involved in founding a platform called ACED which is a platform for design and journalism, so I had the experience of facilitating some sort of a platform where people can come together and have discussions on certain subjects. I felt that the kind of existing spaces to have these conversations and discussions on the Asian diasporas (within and outside of the cultural scene) were too limited, too repetitive, and there were too many expectations of which topics we should be discussing. Therefore, we would like to try to initiate an alternative space for that. We applied to the Stimuleringsfonds with Non Native Native and they were kind enough to support us with a 'startsubsidie' back in 2018. That's when the project kind of launched for the first time. The year after, we started making the research ground more solid and thought of the leading questions we had. Like, what are the Asian narratives, or who are the Asian creatives within the Dutch cultural landscape? As we are two people from Thailand, we cannot really fully represent the Asian communities in The Netherlands. But at least we can bring our knowledge together by getting to know who and where these communities are, and that's how things got started for Non Native Native.

reclaiming the unclaimed

JV   In Non Native Native's mission statement, it says that you wish to "celebrate the art of reclaiming the unclaimed". What is it exactly that you believe is unclaimed? And why should it be reclaimed?

> DT   Essentially we are claiming a space to discuss non-cliché matters. And that is already quite an important step to take, as Asians in the creative industry—or even Asians in general—we are expected to address certain topics in our research and our work. Not so long ago, I was invited to some panel discussion on growing up as a millenial in Asia, and there was a man in the audience who asked me what I thought about communism in China, or, what my opinions were on the communist party in China, something like that. And I was, like, "huh? Is China still a communist country? I don't think so", and also: why am I a representation of China or the Chinese people when I have only been there three times as a tourist. This is one of the many examples

of the expectations that we face, as Asians. People seem to think that Asia is China. And that there is barely any space to go deeper beyond these clichés. So then at some point we were like, "Ok, fuck it, then let's just make the space". To claim a space where we can have conversations about things that matter. So, that is the thing we're claiming.

BP   In addition to that, we are saying 'celebrating': it's a celebration of something that is unclaimed. Unclaimed in the sense that it is an authentic conversation that is not so much happening here, as well as the corresponding conversations or notions that remain untouched. Especially on the point of being Asian living abroad. This notion of something that is in-between, that is almost indescribable even though there are key words such as missing, the sense of belonging, being in-between, the grey area, alien, for example. You cannot even describe if it is Asian experience or not, or Western or not. It is a mix of everything that is coming together because someone who is in a place they are not originally from contains with them a certain sense, certain knowledge, certain cultural background … certain things that might be different to their new environment. But, in a way, instead of feeling trapped in the idea of being "different" or "special", I feel these kinds of qualities can be a contribution to the place in which they are living. The fact that we are sharing these mixed notions that we bring with us can be useful and can be celebrated. And we would like to encourage that to happen much more often.

out-sider from within

JV   In a way, we already touched upon this… but Non Native Native is a cultural platform which looks into the Asian creative landscape in

The Netherlands through the lens of the outsiders from within. Who or what's within? And who or what is (left) outside?

> DT   Well, we are the outsiders, it's essentially that. And we're also operating and navigating within the Dutch creative industry. But then, of course, we will always be the outsider in the Dutch society. Right? I mean, we don't belong here … because we weren't born and raised here, and we don't speak the language. I'm currently learning it, but still. We don't have the same points of cultural reference or upbringing, and that already sets us apart. We can try to integrate, but there's always going to be something that makes us feel that we don't belong.

> BP   I feel like being an outsider is a position that you take. There's also a lot of things that we can choose to not do or do, for example to start learning Dutch and then to go out and be part of certain communities, but we also choose to do something else. To focus on work, to travel, or things like that. There are people who live in Thailand for 10-20 years but they don't understand Thai, and they live in a circle of expats. But there's also people who came from elsewhere who moved to Thailand and they are very integrated into Thai society. They have a Thai family and speak Thai fluently, and you can communicate with them in Thai and they understand all the jokes, so I think it is the position the person chooses to take. And in that sense, to have the lens of the outsider from within, for us, is something to embrace. That this is your own responsibility and choice, and that comes with both the drawback and the benefit of being both. In one way, if we choose to not be an insider, we choose to be an outsider, and maintain a certain set of eyes that are different from someone who is part of it.

When you look from the outside you see things that people who are inside cannot see. Yet you kind of know what's happening because you're on the inside. That is also again the in-between qualities that are a benefit to the communities surrounding it, if you use it wisely or you're willing to embrace that power of being an outsider from within.

JV In NL you speak of the outsider from within, but looking back to your position towards Thailand, do you view that as this kind of insider from the outside? Is that like a reversed dynamic?

BP I think it's the same. Because in Thailand we're also outsiders.

DT Outsiders from inside. I think by being overseas, that already makes us outsiders, in terms of Thailand.

BP I think it's not only about our locations but the fact that we are carrying with us Western belief systems and cultural values, equalities, or hierarchies... What we are used to now, when we carry that back to Thailand, you also need to adjust to how you even talk to your parents, you need to be aware of what you can say, what you can express, and in what way you can say this.

DT We have to bear in mind that there are some very sensitive issues in Thailand. There is a certain self-censorship instinct when you go back.

BP I also think this notion applies to design and design education. I came to know Thai people who came to The Netherlands to study and adopted certain ways of thinking about what design is, or what design can be. Going back to Thailand where the graphic design field is quite strict or limited, they somehow can't survive. They have to fit into that box, system or structure. And I found that really a pity. Because I see a lot of people who have a lot of potential, and if they continue their practice the way they did when they came to study, not only in The Netherlands but also in different places, they would adopt this way of thinking—to explore, to address the things that are important to them. And then once they go back to Thailand there's no space for them to do that. And sometimes it's dangerous for them to do that, so I really admire the people who manage to keep their critical eyes and critical voice within Thailand, because it's a risk, it's a challenge, it needs a lot of art and courage to do it in a way that doesn't get you into too much trouble, whilst also keeping the authenticity of your voice within your own practice.

in-and-out of edu~ca~tion

JV You, Belle, appear to be in-and-out of this educational setting and context. You have your own artistic practice, you co-founded a platform, you teach at the Willem de Kooning Academy. How does this in-and-out of education experience relate to, or expand on the lens of the outsider from within?

BP I think I have been privileged to be able to teach and give lectures to different academies both within The Netherlands and in Thailand. They are totally different experiences—yet, in a way, I have the sense that the qualities of the students, or the ways in which students approach design, is becoming a bit more similar. However, the difference would be what I have already mentioned, which is the environment, or the ecology of what design is in the two countries. Like, here, I would encourage students to be in touch with their subjectivity, to talk about the things that are important to them, valuable to them, to freely express themselves because I know that the environment is safe enough for them to do that. At the end of the day, they will be sent out into the world where they can take care of themselves, and where there is a system that would support what they are doing. But then, within Thailand, I come across students who would like to do similar things, say socially-engaged design and I can guide them to make the best possible production within their education. But afterwards they also ask me about how I make a living out of this kind of work, or how do I make it safe, especially if the work criticises current authority and power structures, and for that I don't have an answer for them. This kind of confinement, or limitation is something that in their future, they know is going to be there, so how are they going to deal with it? I think to engage in more conversations and for the students to be more prepared for their future, is something that I would like to encourage. For example, how do you deal with the ecology that will be different from that you have experienced whilst graduating? Not only in Asia and The Netherlands, but also for someone from other parts of the world. The fact that they go back to their country after graduation, makes it very different from the experience of the people who stay in The Netherlands. This is something that is similar to the conversation we are having, or are trying to have, with Non Native Native.

JV I feel that there is an intrinsic educational element to Non Native Native. How do you view this?

BP We don't consider ourselves to be an educational platform, but, of course, to infiltrate educational systems is our goal. To be able to give a space for people to be able to share and contribute their knowledge is also an education.

DT   Knowledge production and knowledge sharing is a part of education even though it's a very informal way of doing things.

BP   In a way, we don't want to set someone up as an educator and someone else up as a student, or as someone who has to learn. Thinking you have to learn from an Asian person is kind of a strange way to put it. I think there's a difference when you have this conversation within an academy—then this role is very solid. Like someone is teaching something, even though the student can generate a conversation, but at least there still has to be a hierarchical position. Within Non Native Native, everyone is equal. You can teach and you can learn, and you can exchange. And we would also like to keep that notion in all of our activities. We also try to include people from different levels of education, and professional positions, for example, someone who has been in the field for a long time, someone who is an expert, but also young students or someone who has recently graduated, and place them together in a setting where they are equally positioned to share and exchange. That is the plus point of being a platform and not an institution.

non native native fair

JV   You are in the midst of organising the Non Native Native Fair—a 2-day hybrid event that brings together Asian creative cultural practitioners from various backgrounds and disciplines to participate in an experimental, online trade fair environment. The Fair is intended as a platform for observations and expressions of alternative and underrepresented perspectives, especially within the creative industries, where new disciplines and definitions have recently emerged. With this in mind, you have said you would like to create a space for presentation beyond the walls of the galleries, by bringing the show into an experimental trade fair, "where the walls between the creators and audiences are dissolved, where concepts and ideas are made tangible, and commodified to reach the unexpected". Could you expand a little maybe on this sort of deconstructing, or unbuilding of the sturdy gallery walls?

> DT I think it came from this idea that gallery spaces and also institutions are largely very exclusive, right? It attracts a certain type of people and it is made for a certain type of people. It is not made for everyone. And that is the reason for us to decide: we're going to make something, and we want it to be as accessible as possible. In a way that if we change our way of using language, our way of calling things. For example, an exhibition is not an exhibition anymore, but a fair, will that trigger something, or would that attract different, unexpected audiences? So I think it's about the language that we use consciously to make it seem like something more accessible. We don't want to be a white cube. Because we never are, and it's not our thing. By calling it a fair everyone is kind of on an almost equal level. When you think about the architecture of a physical fair, a trade fair, the booth, the market table, the only thing that kind of separates the audience from the performer or the exhibitor is the table, or the line on the floor. But it's not really a physical ... I don't know, I can't articulate it properly right now ...

JV Like not as much a physical obstacle to overcome?

DT   Yes, exactly—there you go: that! There's less of an obstacle. I mean if I tell my grandma we're organising a fair, then she would understand it more than an exhibition. An exhibition and a fair are the same in the way that you are bringing stuff to show to the public. But when you call it an exhibition it creates a different expectation.

JV   And it would attract a different audience perhaps.

BP   We don't know who to expect as an audience, that is also super interesting and exciting. If you are someone within the art and design scenes, you will look at this kind of work from a certain level of understanding and knowledge, but if you then have people who are not familiar with this type of work, and the same work also addresses something sensitive and new … what would be your response? That's also risky in a way. And I appreciate that everyone who is participating is willing to take that risk—bringing out the work and bringing out their own voices. I think it's the same as how people want to go out and protest about racism against Asians, but then they bring their own stories and practices. But that is also what we would like to happen, to have these sorts of conversations beyond the wall of the white walls, beyond the intellectuals, who already have a certain understanding and cope with the situation quite well. If it reaches the kind of people who you should be having the conversation with, about what is Asia or what are the experiences of the Asian diasporas, then that would be something that we aim for, even if it's kind of risky. But we try to keep everything within the umbrella of being as light and fun as possible. We have to see how it goes, but I believe in the community that we have already brought together, this community supports each other and helps each other.

un~~baking~~ a ~~cake~~

JV In my introduction, I touch upon this idea of unbaking a cake—of needing to try out a lot of different ingredients, or recipes to come up with the so-called 'design cake' that it is you wish to (un)bake. Is there something you wish to specifically respond to about the idea of unbaking a cake?

DT I do like the metaphor of unbaking a cake. I never thought about it, but it's definitely not possible scientifically, right?

JV It is definitely scientifically impossible, yes.

[laughing]

BP Maybe I can add something to the notion of the cake. If we consider our practice as baking, I think we are not trying to bake the right cakes but would rather try to find out what the existing cakes around us are and whether they might be authentic or not. Maybe you think: the carrot cake should look and taste like this, but maybe there are a lot of carrot cakes that do not look and taste like the carrot cake you have in mind, but consider themselves carrot cakes nonetheless. Different notions of carrot cakes. And we're not saying this carrot cake is better than this one, or this one is more authentic than this one, or this one came from The Netherlands and this one came from somewhere else—to us they're all considered carrot cakes. Non Native Native is looking into different relations of that type of cake, and we would just like to give our audience, or ourselves, the knowledge and a choice, to suggest: "Hey there are varieties of carrot cakes out there which you can look into. Maybe you don't agree that it is a carrot cake, but it is there." Maybe you would unexpectedly appreciate this type of carrot cake with a strawberry on top that you didn't know existed. And maybe some carrot cakes work here, and others in other parts of the world.

> DT   No carrot cakes are wrong. There's no distinction to us—they're all carrot cakes, they're all the same, they're just different, but they might share something similar. We're not in the position to say what's right and what's wrong either, we don't want to judge who's in and who's out, for example.

BP   It is up to the person in the location to judge the carrot cake. If we export this particular cake that is so popular in one area to another ecology, or ecological setting, maybe no one will care. And vice versa. Maybe no one cares about it in a certain location but then in another location, suddenly it's gold. Your metaphor makes me think a little bit more about how what we're doing can be more about the discovery of different types of variations, and to see how things, when they are placed differently, or valued differently, adapt to that ecology to be a popular cake or to be a cake that functions within the cultural scene. How do we frost the cake in a way that it contributes to the cultural landscape? These kinds of things. That is what we're interested in.

> DT   Once the cake is made, it is out there. In a way, it's like knowledge—once you learn it, it's there. You can't get rid of it, you can't unsee it. I think it's also like this with the different varieties of cakes; now that we know they exist, we cannot say they do not exist anymore. They now need to be swallowed and digested.

105

a disappointing bibliography

Teaching Design

A disappointing bibliography

What should we teach? How should we teach? Whom are we teaching? What does "teaching" mean anyway, and how are we positioning ourselves within institutional teaching contexts? Those questions (among others) came up in a very practical sense when we—Lisa and Judith—started teaching design. Lisa teaches design theory and practice at universities in Germany, whereas Judith teaches at an MBO, which is vocational education, in the Netherlands. Although we have been teaching in very different contexts, we found many similarities within the institutions we are part of: a eurocentric, male dominated canon, strict hierarchies, little awareness of pedagogical and intersectional discourses and practices, precarious contracts, rigid institutional structures and time limitations.

      With only a few like-minded educators within reach at that time, we turned to papers, books, lectures, podcasts and websites for answers. We discovered that we were certainly not the first to think about these topics. The resources we collected helped us in navigating our fields, whilst empowering us and allowing us to become allies along the way.

      Inspired by Sarah Ahmed's "survival toolkit for feminist killjoys" in *Living A Feminist Life* (2017), the following resources have accompanied us, guided us and picked us up during the past years' experiences in design education. They ultimately found their way into our bibliography. The following list is flexible, expandable and has no claim to being complete or final. We rather hope the following suggestions act as an entry point, as well as encouragement, to pause and reflect and then to look further, to stay curious and care-ful. As Elena Garfinkel writes: "Lists will always disappoint, even as they promise an inexhaustible world, an infinite plenum". So, we sure hope to disappoint.

Anja Kaiser and Rebecca Stephany (ed.)
Glossary of Undisciplined Design
Spector Books, 2021

Anna Wahl
The Cloud – Lecturing on feminist research
NORA nos. 2–3 1999, Volume 7, p. 97–108.
https://www.researchgate.net/publication/233313068_The_Cloud_-_Lecturing_on_feminist_research

bell hooks
Understanding Patriarchy
https://imaginenoborders.org/pdf/zines/UnderstandingPatriarchy.pdf

Catherine Denial
A Pedagogy of Kindness
In: Jesse Stommel, Chris Friend, Sean Michael Morris (eds.): Critical Digital Pedagogy. A collection.
Hybrid Pedagogy, 2020

Chimamanda Ngozi Adichie
The danger of a single story
TED Global 2009
https://www.ted.com/talks/chimamanda_ngozi_adichie_the_danger_of_a_single_story?language=de

Dori Tunstall
Decolonising Design
Berkeley Talks. Episode 12, 30.01.2019.
https://news.berkeley.edu/2019/01/25/berkeley-talks-dori-tunstall/

何穎雅 Elaine W. Ho & 吴索 Amy Suo Wu
Radio Slumber
https://www.radioslumber.net/

Elena Gorfinkel
Against Lists
Another Gaze, 2019
https://www.anothergaze.com/elena-gorfinkel-manifesto-against-lists/

Gurminder K. Bhambra, Dalia Gebrial and Kerem Nişancıoğlu (Eds.)
Decolonising the University
London, Pluto Press, 2018
https://library.oapen.org/bitstream/id/0b692853-23af-49ad-83a9-6844dca1dc1d/1004145.pdf

Jacob Lindgren
Graphic Design's Factory Settings
The Gradient – Walker Arts Center. Jan 2, 2020.
https://walkerart.org/magazine/jacob-lindgren-graphic-designs-factory-settings

KUNCI Study Forum & Collective
The classroom is burning, let's dream about a School of Improper Education
Ugly Duckling Presse, 2020
https://uglyducklingpresse.org/publications/letters-the-classroom-is-burning/

Leana Boven en Sayonara Stutgard (ed.)
Aether, essays over zorg en samenzijn
NL: *https://thisismama.nl/invest/webshop/aether/*
EN: *https://thisismama.nl/en/invest/webshop-en/aether/*

Nora Sternfeld
Wessen Kultur und wessen Bildung?
ZfK – Zeitschrift für Kulturwissenschaften 2|2019
https://www.uni-muenster.de/Ejournals/index.php/ZfK/article/view/2527/2405

Sara Ahmed
Complaint as diversity work
CRASSH Impact Lecture Series, 9.3.2018
https://www.youtube.com/watch?v=JQ_1kFwkfVE&t=1527s

> **Simpson Tse**
> **Care, the Friendly Ghost**
> **Thesis, Sandberg Instituut, 2020**
> *https://sandberg.nl/thesis/simpson-tse*
>
> ...

biographies

Biographies

Saskia van Stein is an independent curator, moderator, and educator, whose work places an emphasis on design and architecture. She has been Head of Department of the MA entitled The Critical Inquiry Lab, a department with artistic (design) research at its core, since 2019. The course provides an environment for the development of a design practice that is understood as a cultural signifier and an agent of change. Van Stein was Director at Bureau Europa, platform for architecture and design, in Maastricht (2013–2019), she worked as a curator at the Netherlands Architecture Institute (now Het Nieuwe Instituut) in Rotterdam (2003–2012) and contributes to the development of cultural discourse as a board member of multiple advisory committees. She is also involved in several juries and advisory bodies such as The Independent School for the City and the architectural peer to peer review journal OASE. Besides her work as Head of Department at the Design Academy, she is a PhD candidate at the Curatorial Research Community at the Technical University of Eindhoven.

> Nadine Botha is a curator, editor, writer, reader, watcher, listener, student, curator and poet. She has worked for Design Indaba, Mail&Guardian and VISI, and written for the FT, Metropolis, Coolhunting, Design Observer, Core 77, Art South Africa and Chimurenga, among others. In her work, Nadine focuses on the unseen social, political, economic, scientific and cultural values embedded in our material reality. Her work explores how these values design our objects, bodies, homes, cities, technologies, experiences and knowledges. In 2018 she co-curated the 4th Istanbul Design Biennial—A School of Schools.

Alice Twemlow's research addresses design's complex interrelations with time and the environment and manifests in writing, exhibitions, conferences, and education. She is Research Professor at the Royal

Academy of Art, The Hague (KABK) where she leads the "Design and the Deep Future" readership, and an Associate Professor at Leiden University, in the Academy for Creative and Performing Arts, where she supervises design-related PhDArts candidates. Previously, Alice was head of the Design Curating & Writing Master at Design Academy Eindhoven, and before that she lived in New York where, in 2008, she co-founded and directed the MFA in Design Criticism (D-Crit), and then the MA in Design Research, Writing & Criticism, at the School of Visual Arts. Alice has a PhD and an MA in the History of Design from the Royal College of Art/Victoria & Albert Museum, London, and she now lives in Amsterdam with her husband, son, and dog.

Imad Gebrayel is a Lebanese designer, educator and researcher based in Berlin. He has produced visual and theoretical works around self-Orientalism in Arab design, counter-mapping and archiving. He also collaborated with several journalistic platforms, exploring common grounds between design and media outlets across Europe. With several years of experience as creative director between Abu Dhabi and Beirut, he moved to the Netherlands, where he received a Master's degree in Design. He then moved to Berlin where he co-founded the Queer Arab Barty. Gebrayel is currently teaching at several academic institutions, and undertaking ethnographic research on the negotiations of Arab-Muslim identifications in the context of Sonnenallee as part of his PhD project at the Institute for European Ethnology at Humboldt University Berlin. His project stems from notions of difference within the presumed sameness of the Arab immigrant in Berlin and aims at informing research on gender, class and memory in the field.

(she/her) Maya Ober is is a designer, researcher, educator, writer, and activist based in Basel, Switzerland. She holds a B.Des. in industrial design from Holon Institute of Technology and an MA in Design Research from Berne University of the Arts. Maya is the founder of depatriarchise design. She works as a research associate at the Institute of Industrial Design and as a lecturer at the Institute of Aesthetic Practice and Theory at the Academy of Arts and Design in Basel. There, together with Laura Pregger she has developed the educational programme "Imagining Otherwise", looking at how intersectionality can inform design practice. Maya is also a co-head of "Educating Otherwise" – a continuing education programme for design educators at the FHNW Academy of Art and Design in Basel.

> depatriarchise design is a feminist community and design research platform working across different mediation formats. Their manifold investigative and activist practice is rooted in intersectional feminism. Founded in 2017, depatriarchise design was born out of frustration with a design discipline that is deeply interwoven with discriminating structures. depatriarchise design started as a call for action. The urgency for change in design practice and its dominant paradigms is their driving force. Through texts, workshops, and exhibitions, depatriarchise design examine the complicity of design in the reproduction of oppressive systems, but also tell long-silenced stories. Constantly researching feminist pedagogies, they stir alternative modes of teaching design, initiating workshops, and bringing people together to learn from and with each other.

Born in Bangkok in 1984, Belle Phromchanya was trained as a graphic designer before relocating to Amsterdam in 2011 to study MA Design at the Sandberg Instituut. Today, she continues her artistic practice between The Netherlands and Thailand. Her works address subjects such as political memeification, digital legacy, marginalized-transborder identities, and contemporary migration, many of which are rooted in the unsettling relationship between herself and the globalized society. The projects are made up of visual research, information graphics, multimedia installation, and audiovisual production, displaying personal exploration of the current reality.

Darunee Terdtoontaveedej (1990) is a curator and researcher with a strong interest in collecting and forming a collection. Trained as an architect at Central Saint Martins College of Art and Design, University of the Arts London, and, later, as a designer at Design Academy Eindhoven, Terdtoontaveedej specialises in cross-disciplinary collaboration and looking beyond the design world. Her fascinations include issues such as the home and senses of belonging, the selves, and alternative histories. Prior to her Masters education in The Netherlands, she worked as a design and architecture journalist and editor for art4d magazine, Thailand's first design magazine and book publisher. Since 2019, she has been the LGBTQ+ programme curator at CinemAsia Film Festival, and, in 2020, was selected as the Young Curator of the 49th edition of International Film Festival Rotterdam (IFFR).

Non Native Native (NNN) is a cultural platform which looks into the Asian creative landscape in The Netherlands through the lens of the outsiders from within. The platform serves as an alternative point of exchange for critical creative practitioners between the Asian and Dutch cultural landscape with a focus on contemporary visual cultures. The initiative was formed in late 2018, and through a series of research and public activities, they aim to combine the contemporary work of Asian creatives with local diaspora narratives, bringing to the surface a nuanced representation of Asian visibility in popular culture. They aim to construct an alternative speculation—or rather—impression on the world's future, through critical reflection of Asian actors who are part of the global cultural landscape. Non Native Native is co-founded by designers and curators: Belle Phromchanya, Darunee Terdtoontaveedej, and Honey Kraiwee, and operates in collaboration with diverse professionals to celebrate the art of reclaiming the unclaimed.

Teaching Design started as a collectively gathered bibliography focusing on design education from intersectional feminist and decolonial perspectives. Since its launch in September 2019, it has expanded into conversational formats, workshops, a temporary library and a space for reflections, all of which have led to the platform in its current form. Teaching Design invites design educators, students, alumni, faculty staff and everyone interested in the field to share experiences, doubts, questions, knowledge, concepts, methods and references, and to connect, reflect and learn collectively. Teaching Design aims to collect resources that could function as reference points and/or inspiration to (educational) practices. As a participative format, Teaching Design is constantly in transition, welcoming proposals for collaborations of any kind. Teaching Design is currently led by Lisa Baumgarten and Judith Leijdekkers.

Lot Mars is a conceptual graphic designer with a great interest in language. She completed a bachelor's degree in Graphic Design (Willem de Kooning Academy, Rotterdam) and a master's degree in Communication & Cognition (Tilburg University). Her visual work is minimalistic and stems from the true essence of a product or concept. By exploring how existing concepts can be represented, re-described, or viewed differently, she strives to expose the unseen. Lot Mars is also the designer of the Stotts typeface—a written form of stuttering: an award-winning typeface that raises awareness and deepens the public's understanding towards stuttering.

Wibke Bramesfeld (1992, DE) is an independent graphic and communication designer, based in Rotterdam, NL. Wibke studied at the Peter Behrens School of Arts in Düsseldorf, DE (2012–2016), HDK – Academy of Design and Crafts, Göteborg, SE (2014–2015), and received her MA from the department 'Information Design' at Design Academy Eindhoven, NL, in 2019. Since then she has been running her own design practice 'Studio Bramesfeld'. The studio focuses on book design, visual communication, and graphic identities, across the cultural field at large. The approach of Studio Bramesfeld's work is not only to create visually stimulating designs, but to also build conceptually strong foundations, by taking elements such as graphic design, typography, colour, and materials into consideration for each individual project. The studio has worked in collaboration with many cultural organisations and art publishers, including Valiz, nai010, Archiprix, Design Academy Eindhoven, Onomatopee Projects, and PrintRoom.

Joannette van der Veer is an independent design curator and writer based in Rotterdam. She holds an MA in Design Cultures from the Vrije Universiteit Amsterdam and a BA in Design from the Willem de Kooning Academy Rotterdam. Curiosity, criticism, collaboration and conviviality are the core principles of her hybrid creative practice that spans across the field of art and design(ed) cultures. Previous publications include *CriticAll!* and *Design in Conservative Times* (both published by Onomatopee Projects), of which she was the editor / curator at large. She has worked for a variety of cultural institutions in The Netherlands, including Transnatural Art & Design, Roodkapje Rotterdam, Niet Normaal Foundation and Onomatopee Projects.

colophon

Colophon

onomatop-ee 206
unununimimimdededesign
—the hesitant state of design

isbn
978-94-93148-89-5

editor
Joannette van der Veer

contributing authors
Saskia van Stein
Nadine Botha
Alice Twemlow
Imad Gebrayel
Maya Ober (depatriarchise design)
Belle Phromchanya (Non Native Native)
Darunee Terdtoontaveedej (Non Native Native)
Lisa Baumgarten (Teaching Design)
Judith Leijdekkers (Teaching Design)
Joannette van der Veer

text editor
Amy Gowen

graphic design
Cover: Lot Mars
Inside: Studio Bramesfeld

fonts
stotts by Lot Mars
Söhne by Klim type Foundry

paper
Cover: 265 g/m² Wibalin Natural Strongboard
Inside: 120 g/m² Circle Offset Premium White

printer
Drukkerij Tielen

special thanks to

The participants and alumni of The Critical Inquiry Lab: Viktória Kaslik, Cecilia Casabona, Lara Chapman, Maxime Benvenuto, Josh Plough, Fernand Bretillot, Ramón Jimenez Cardenas, Janfer Chung, Tiiu Meiner and Sofia Irene Marmolejo Bijnsdorp for their contribution to Saskia & Nadine's contribution; Rana Ghavami and her students for sharing thoughts, ideas and feedback; Anja Kaiser and Rebecca Stephany for an insightful conversation; and all the other engaged individuals involved in the process of developing this publication.

made possible by

Creative Industries Fund NL
Province of Noord-Brabant

creative industries fund NL

Provincie Noord-Brabant

Onomatopee and authors © 2022

All rights reserved. No part of this publication may be reproduced, stored in a retrieval system, or transmitted in any form or by any means, electronic, mechanical, photocopied, recorded or otherwise, without the prior written permission from the authors and the publisher.

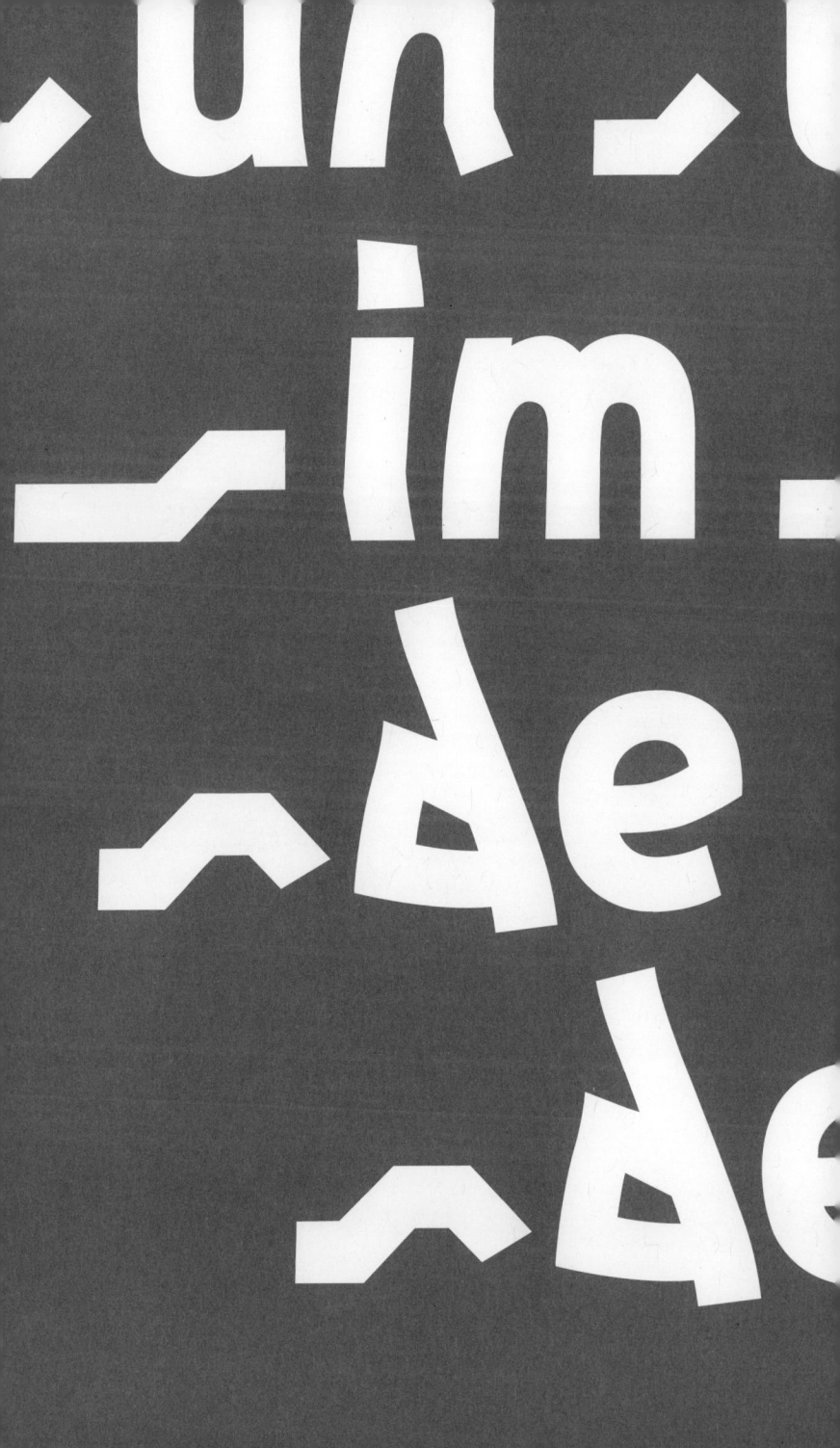

un_un
_im_
_de_
esign

h un
m i
e de
desig

fun in de design